CHRISTIAN POLITICAL ACTION
in an
AGE OF REVOLUTION

CHRISTIAN POLITICAL ACTION *in an* *AGE OF REVOLUTION*

Guillaume Groen van Prinsterer

Colin Wright, *translator*

WordBridge
PUBLISHING
εν αρχη ην ο λογος
AALTEN, THE NETHERLANDS

WORDBRIDGE PUBLISHING
Aalten, the Netherlands
www.wordbridge.net

French original: *Le parti Anti-revolutionnaire et Confessionnel dans l'Église Reforméé des Pays-Bas: Etude d'histoire contemporaine,* 1860.

Copyright © 2015 Ruben Alvarado
ISBN 978-90-76660-44-8 (paperback)

Cover illustration: Eugène Delacroix, *La liberté guidant le people* [Liberty Guides the People], Musée du Louvre, Paris. The painting commemorates the so-called "July Revolution" of 1830. Source: Wikimedia Commons—"This work is in the public domain in its country of origin and other countries and areas where the copyright term is the author's life plus 100 years or less."

TABLE OF CONTENTS

Notes on the Translation v
Publisher's Foreword vii
Preface xv
I. The Orthodox Confessional Party 1
    The ultraorthodox circle in the Walloon community in The Hague 1
    My portrait 6
    The confessional party in the Reformed Church 12
    Its principles with respect to the creeds 15
    The orthodoxy of Dordt 21
    Our attitude towards dissent, rationalism in the church, the theological faculties, and primary education 25
    The nature and scope of our defence of the church's rights in the States General 32
    Confusion of church and state? 35
II. The Anti-Revolutionary Principle 39
    What is the Revolution? 39
    Its history 42
    Anarchistic contradictions 49
    Witnesses old and new 52
    The lessons of modern history 55
    Contemporary anti-revolutionary writers 61
    The anti-revolutionary principle is none other than the Christian principle 73
    Ultramontanism cannot successfully combat the Revolution .. 79
    The Reformation alone is capable of defeating the Revolution, provided it remains faithful to the Gospel and thereby confronts modern thought 88
    Pseudo-conservatism 96
    Conservation and progress 99
III. Our Parliamentary Opposition 105
    An opposition of principles 105
    The constitution and its organic laws 108
    Many and varied opponents 114
    Chances of success 118
    Our party's influence increases 124
    How to explain the disappointing result of our action— and yet, no reason for despair 131
Index 137

NOTES ON THE TRANSLATION

Text in square brackets may indicate several things: either the original word (in cases in which different interpretations of the word are possible), or the translation of a book or article title, or an interpolation by the translator or editor. Footnotes in the original text were entirely inadequate to modern scholarly standards, and therefore have been thoroughly reworked. Similarly, errors in the text have been tacitly corrected. Finally, the method of quotation did not always come up to modern scientific standards; we have done our best to bring them to those standards.

PUBLISHER'S FOREWORD

This is a description and defence of Christian politics. The writer, Guillaume Groen van Prinsterer (1801–1876) was a pioneer in this area, a leading Dutch politician and head of the Anti-Revolutionary Party, which he created.

The son of a medical doctor, Groen enjoyed a classical education and gained a reputation as an outstanding practitioner of languages, especially Latin.[1] He received doctorates in both law and letters at the University of Leyden, and soon thereafter became a member of King William I's cabinet. As the Netherlands and Belgium were then one country, he relocated to the court in Brussels with his newlywed bride in 1828. This was momentous for his further development: he there met proponents of the Christian revival movement known as the Réveil,[2] chiefly the court preacher J.H. Merle d'Aubigné. At this point his views shifted from a middle-of-the-road latitudinarian liberal Christianity to a committed Reformed orthodoxy, and he became a champion of the Dutch Reformed Church and the House of Orange. And his writing began to reflect that. He was appointed archivist of the royal archives, the volumes of which, published under his direction, lent him international fame. While continuing with his literary efforts he also entered into politics, forming the Anti-Revolutionary Party as one of the major factions in the Lower House of the States General, the Netherlands' legislative body.

Groen established this party to oppose the revolutionary movement that began with the French Revolution in 1789 and continued in various iterations throughout the 19th century.

---

[1]These biographical notes are derived mainly from the entry written by Alexander de Savornin Lohman in the *Nieuw Nederlandsch biografisch woordenboek. Deel 2* [New Dutch Biographical Dictionary, vol. 2] (Leyden: A.W. Sijthoff, 1912), pp. 508–520.
[2]The Réveil was a 19th-century revivalist movement that mainly impacted Protestantism in France, Switzerland, and the Netherlands.

This revolutionary movement was after more than just a change in leadership or reworking of institutions: it was a fundamental attack on the spiritual basis of Western civilisation, quite simply, the enthronement of man in place of God. "In its essence, the Revolution is a single great historical fact: the invasion of the human mind by the doctrine of the absolute sovereignty of man, thus making him the source and centre of all truth, by substituting human reason and human will for divine revelation and divine law. The Revolution is the history of the irreligious philosophy of the past century; it is, in its origin and outworking, the doctrine that—given free rein—destroys church and state, society and family, produces disorder without ever establishing liberty or restoring moral order, and, in religion, inevitably leads its conscientious followers into atheism and despair" (p. 40).

Hence the need for a Christian politics. But what is that? Certainly not the modern sort of politics, which demands compromise of principles in order to share power; rather, it is the transcendent sort, where principle is placed over expediency. As such, this book explains the necessity for Christianity in the public arena. For Christianity is a statement regarding the ultimate source of law and authority, and if Christianity does not posit this, some other religion will, even the religion of autonomous man, who knows no authority over himself, making himself the law.

So then, the state *needs* Christianity. "At this level, the struggle of both is against the same doctrine, one that is equally destructive of church and state, that is, of morality and law. We need to be aware of this connection and not attempt to sunder what are indissoluble bonds. We do not thereby sacrifice religion to politics, or politics to religion. Neither do we paralyse the living regenerative forces of society, or erect a barrier against the spirit of improvement and progress. Quite the contrary. We thereby ensure religion its rightful influence. We bestow on an enlightened politics a renewed vision" (p. 98).

On all sides one hears objections to Christian involvement in the public arena. But this involvement does not constitute the unwarranted mingling of church and state. Nor does it necessarily involve a descent into the horse-trading compromises of typical party politics. Christian politics is principled and prophetic; it is the reign of truth over opinion. "We are not a shade of opinion that with other shades of opinion make up a single party; we are a separate party in our own right; we are bound together by fundamental yet neglected verities, and by a *principle* that is opposed to a whole array of *opinions* that—whatever differences they might have or appear to have—are united in a common contempt for what we regard as the indispensable condition for social order" (p. 98).

Liberalism hides behind democracy to obscure the true import of what it is about. But democracy is not necessarily a vehicle of liberalism. "Christianity can work with democracy as with any other form of government. But if it is imposed as an absolute and necessary condition of the social order, hailed as a revolutionary dogma, and opposed to God's law—whose eternal authority must be respected by every sovereign power, be it popular or regal—the democracy of the social contract will always find itself opposed by the Christian faith" (p. 74).

Today's Christians have forgotten these truths. They think they can get by, by accepting the presuppositions of liberalism and simply moderating the practice thereof. But this is a path leading to destruction, for practice will increasingly realise principle, and when that happens, there will be no more room for escape. "It is regrettable that, even today, many Christians, disillusioned by the promises of liberalism, nevertheless believe that they can take on board its principles, in whole or in part, to serve the cause of religion and freedom. It is regrettable that they have not discovered, under the misleading veil of seeming moderation, the identity of principle with a radicalism that strikes at the very heart of religion and society, and thus making them the blind instruments of 'the hidden power that irresistibly draws the consequences from the principle, never suspecting that they are engaged in its fatal development'" (p. 72).

Indeed, there is peculiar blindness that afflicts Christians when it comes to recognising what is at stake in the current situation of cultural warfare. Going along to get along seemed to work for a while, but the time comes when it no longer does so. So why do Christians continue to delude themselves as to the gravity of the situation? "Now, why—after having wholeheartedly embraced evangelical beliefs—why do they not see that the prevailing spirit of our times has its origin and raison d'être in a rejection of *revealed* truth?

"Why do they not see that the overthrow of the religious, political, and social order was not the result of a revolutionary *blip*, but of a revolutionary *condition*, and that *perpetual revolution* always has been and always will be the inevitable consequence of the denial of man's dependence on the God of nature, history and the Gospel?

"Why do they not see that this evil cannot be brought to an end by attacking merely its symptoms? It has to be torn up by the roots.

"Why do they not see that the only antidote for systematic unbelief is faith?

"Why do they not see that the anti-revolutionary principle is nothing other than the Protestant Christian principle, the *Reformation* principle? It alone—*standing on revelation and history*—can successfully combat this anti-religious, anti-social principle. It alone, *through the Gospel*, can realise whatever there is of truth and goodness in these revolutionary utopias, and so save both church and state" (p. 39).

But is this not a recipe for intolerance? Does not liberalism promote tolerance and respect for all views? This objection misconstrues what the tolerance agenda is all about. It is not about equality of viewpoints, but about the elimination of viewpoints that claim to represent the truth: tolerance is *intolerant of absolute truth* (as if a qualifier is needed! But such is the condition of our relativistic modernist mindset, that such qualifiers are in fact needed to make clear what one means). "When we exclude *no* opinion, by the same token we exclude every *exclusive* opinion; the truth, the Gospel, has no place in this syncretism. Tolerance of erroneous opinions can only be provisional or exceptional; for where error is allowed free rein, truth becomes a seed of confusion, and can only be accommodated by denying its nature and obligations and leaving error in peace" (p. 18).

The modern Christian retorts, "We cannot return to the days of divine right!" But does he even know what the words mean? Is divine right a formula for absolute monarchy? Not quite: "*Divine right:* but not in the sense of a Jewish theocracy, nor in the absurd sense of the Stuarts, nor in the sense of Hobbes' servility, nor yet as interpreted by Bonaparte. Rather, we mean divine right as it was understood before the advent of the Revolution: as the basis of all government, republican or monarchical, and as the only adequate foundation for every right and every liberty" (p. 50).

What is involved here? Nothing less than the sovereignty of God! Christian, do you believe in that? "We have to choose between the sovereignty of man and the sovereignty of God. Reject sovereignty by the grace of God and you are left with nothing but radicalism. Without divine right, there is no genuine authority, whether kingly, parliamentary or republican; these names offer nothing but a state of revolution, where force upholds one party and puts down another, while being itself at every turn the central power. There is no other option: you can have anarchy and servitude as the products of a social contract, or you can find the source of rights and liberty in the absolute and beneficial authority of God" (p. 51).

The sovereignty of God has its corollary in the recognition of the church as the body of Christ, who is the Son of God and King of Kings. "And [the Father] put all things in subjection under [the Son's] feet, and gave Him as head over all things to the church, which is His body, the fullness of Him who fills all in all" (Ephesians 1:22–23). The church has a crucial role to play in the furtherance of God's Kingdom on earth. Therefore, the subjection of the church by the state is a condition that cannot be tolerated: but it was the reality in the 19th century

Netherlands. The constitutional arrangement had made the church of a department of state with no room for independent action. Instead, a government-appointed bureaucracy dictated its range of activity. "Against what have we constantly protested? Against an arbitrary regime that, with illusory promises of a future separation, continues to impose its very real yoke; against an organisation of the church that is contrary to its principles and traditions; against its subjugation under oligarchic forms; against its identification with this governmental straitjacket; against the government's conduct in making common cause with the enemies of the church, who are protected by regulatory provisions and are past masters of insolent attack and underhand scheming" (p. 32).

Why was this important? Because, as the church in the West has always realised, it is *libertas ecclesiae,* the freedom of the church, which underlies all social and political freedom. A church subordinated to the whims of a government bureaucracy is a church in Babylonian captivity, not in freedom. It is from the church that the bulwarks and the ramparts come forth that thwart the advance of the forces of Revolution. For it is Reformation, not Revolution, that the nations have need of. Reformation preserves and builds, winnows and harvests, while Revolution crushes and destroys, eliminates all source of prosperity and progress, and levels society to a grey inert mass of mediocrity. "The situation in France and across Europe called loudly for a reformation. But it did not make desirable or even inevitable the very opposite of a reformation: an anti-religious revolution, a revolution in the fundamental ideas of social order; one that overthrows—under the guise of reforming abuse—even the most useful institutions, and one that denies—under the guise of combatting prejudice—even the most sacred principles" (p. 46).

The ministry of the church extends to the fields of education and poor relief: another truth that has been forgotten in the blind acceptance of the role of the state as exclusive purveyor of public goods, the loss of which has engendered a grand transmission belt for the furtherance of liberal domination, allowing liberalism to sink its teeth ever deeper into the electorate. Yes, these goods are public, but they do not fall under the exclusive jurisdiction of the state. And Christians having abandoned these fields to "public [i.e., government] schools," to "philanthropy," to "welfare," have done the church a great disservice. "Education and charity: these domains belong to the church, or at the very least the state should not lay claim to them as its own. It cannot set itself up as sole teacher and grand almoner of the nation without stripping the church of its rights and duties. What we have here are simple corollaries of the spiritual power's nature and mission, and every church in which a living heart beats has always resisted the usurpations of the secular arm on these great issues" (p. 35).

Government policy needs to be radically revised, recognising the diaconal ministry of the church, indeed the church's right and duty to administer these public goods. "Similarly, on the issue of poverty, we felt that the state should not only respect the independence of the churches, but that it should also acknowledge their support; that Christian charity should not be regulated, nor its streams of benevolence dried up by public assistance; that systematic taxation for the sake of the poor should be rigorously eschewed, and pauperism should not be made the object of the public purse by recognising, at least indirectly, a right to the state's assistance" (p. 35). For this only foments the spirit of entitlement, that bane of every democratic regime, as Thomas Chalmers elsewhere so eloquently declaimed.

A recovery of the church is the top priority of a truly Christian politics. The restored church provides the anchor for politics generally, not for any specific party. "This regenerated church, in my opinion, must not become the tool of a political party. It must become the leaven spoken of in the parable: the only genuine means of advancing the kingdom of God in every sphere of life" (p. 103).

Christians need to come to grips with the reality of the Revolution. Given the positive result of the American Revolution, the word has managed to retain a favourable connotation. But even the American Revolution had its dark side: the gradual yet decisive elimination of the church from public life. It is time that Christians realise that this was no advance, nor was it an improvement, but rather the delivery of the rule of law into the hands of autonomous man. "The Revolution is simply the systematic undermining of the church of Jesus Christ; and a genuinely anti-revolutionary resistance to it is simply a perpetual witness to the Faith, in a form dictated by our time. It is the Christian principle in its lawful, necessary and timely application" (p. 73).

All of this leads to a single ineluctable conclusion: our world is careening toward Armageddon, as the forces of autonomous man demand ever more control of and sovereignty over all of life, public and private, family and church, reaching even to the level of thought and conscience. The sooner Christians wake up to this fundamental reality, the sooner they will allow themselves to be used by God, as witnesses, prophets, and martyrs, in the midst of a wicked and perverse generation. The political struggle is a spiritual struggle, a war of religion. "What is after all, speaking religiously, the great question, the most important question which at present occupies the minds of men? It is the question in debate between those who acknowledge and those who deny a supernatural, certain, and sovereign order of things, although inscrutable to human reason. The question in dispute, to call things by their right names, between supernaturalism and naturalism. On the one side, unbelievers, pantheists, pure rationalists, and sceptics of all kinds. On the other, Christians. Amongst the first, the best still allow to the statue of the Deity, if I may make use of such an expression, a place in the world and in the human soul; but to the statue only,—an image, a marble. God himself is no longer there. Christians alone possess the living God" (p. 78). And they had better get ready to confess Him, no matter the price.

PREFACE

My reason for publishing this study is the desire to provide our Christian friends in Switzerland, France and elsewhere with information about the current situation in the Dutch Reformed Church, particularly with regard to the views and labours of the party to which I have the honour of belonging—known as the *confessional* party, and as often referred to as the *orthodox* or *Anti-Revolutionary Party*.

While it might appear impossible at the present time to resolve the confusion that reigns among us, or the deplorable consequences it has for the nation's religious and moral interests, I do not believe that this impossibility is on the whole the result of serious differences, among those who are united by the bond of faith and have long marched together in fraternal agreement, about the nature of the church.

In 1856, at the height of the crisis brought on by the re-organisation of primary education—at precisely that moment when everything seemed to point to imminent success—we were forsaken by many who had previously made common cause with us. The consequences of this regrettable split were not long in surfacing. A year later, in 1857, a law was passed that outlawed all expression of Christianity in the public schools, established mixed schools, and declared a strict neutrality with respect to all religions, existing and imaginary. It dashed our hopes and rendered all our efforts useless.

After such a disappointment, which all at once rendered me inactive and returned me to private life, I withdrew into historical research. I was only too happy to continue with the publication of the archives of the House of Orange with renewed zeal, and studiously avoid controversy. Such a bitter experience, I told myself, may (by leading us to re-think) be the means of reconciliation and turn to our advantage. But if we were to achieve this goal, and come to a mutual and just appreciation of our conduct and motives, it was vital that we did not return to squabbling. We had to avoid impassioned reproaches and recriminations. We had to give, and be given by, our opponents, time for serious and quiet reflection; and thus to aspire to consider our own actions and those of others with the severe impartiality of a judge and the trained eye of an historian.

Those who abandoned us at the crucial moment have not seen fit to pursue such a course. On the contrary; the more the consequences of our disunity have unfolded, the more effort they have made to shift the whole responsibility for it onto the confessional party. The irreligious reaction—which now threatens us on all sides—is, we are assured, nothing but the natural and inevitable result of our exaggeration, our narrowness, our intolerance, our antiquated views, our outdated mentality, our numerous shortcomings, the manner in which we engaged in warfare and sought strife, our commitment to a creed long since out of touch with the times, and our propensity to confuse religion and politics. Disunity, they add, is certainly regrettable; but to have persisted with a false and dangerous system would have been even more fatal. If we complain, they gasp at our stubbornness and exclaim: It was only by a frank disapproval of your principles and actions that your better-informed friends, by keeping quiet about their sympathies, were able to protect themselves and you from complete disgrace, and secure opportunities for the future.

At the time, an immediate response to these repeated affronts and attacks did not seem necessary. We felt justified in relying on the memory of our compatriots, and their being able to compare past criticisms of all shades with the testimony of their own recent recollections. This is no longer the case: they have now gone beyond our borders, and promulgated inaccurate views of our opinions and aims among those who are not in a position to judge for themselves, and who would thus be inclined to put a disadvantageous construction on our dogged silence.

This is why, despite my reluctance to enter the lists, I came to the conclusion that I could no longer refrain from putting pen to paper, when judgement was passed on us in an article that provoked general consternation: *Quelques mots sur l'état religieux de la Hollande* [A few words about the religious situation in Holland], published on 25 October 1859 by the Lausanne magazine *Le Chrétien Évangélique du 19ᵉ siècle* [The Evangelical Christian in the Nineteenth Century].

The article was by Mr Trottet,[3] a pastor at The Hague since 1858. He expresses himself very unfavourably with regard to the orthodox party in the Dutch Reformed Church, the ultraorthodox circle of the Walloon community of The Hague, and not least my own prejudices: my obstinate adherence to a system incompatible with the needs of the time, the affinity of my ideas with Puseyism, my inability to embrace the path of real progress, and my refusal to examine things with a view to extracting what is good in them. Since I had complete confidence in his intentions and character, I would have preferred to wait patiently for a deeper knowledge to lead the author himself to publicly modify his opinion. As he had only recently arrived in the country, it was only to be expected that he would make serious mistakes by giving a hasty account of an extremely complex religious state of affairs. Added to which, I was inclined to trust that, when he came to realise that his assessment, even from his own perspective, was unjust and exaggerated, he would speedily rectify his error.[4] Here's what persuaded me

---

[3] Jean-Pierre Trottet (1818–1862), Swiss clergyman and theologian.

[4] [Written by Groen:] Sadly, I can find nothing resembling such a confession in the first part of a larger work by Mr Trottet in *La Revue Chrétien* [The Christian Journal] of May 15 entitled "La question religieuse en Hollande" [The religious question in Holland]. I believe he should have seized this opportunity to make amends to a section of his community. Besides, I am pleased to see here, much more than in the previous article, his trepidation at being unfair to me. As for any observations I might make, I could hardly do other than repeat what I have previously said in a work I am about to present to the Christian public. I trust it will lead some to question what Mr Trottet has affirmed, namely, that the party which (he says) still counts me among its members (and which he calls the pure orthodox wing) "undoubtedly constitutes a retrograde party that serves only to increase the perils of the situation, by provoking

to take a different tack, when I reread his account. To whom, I asked myself, to whom—since he knew neither the facts nor the circumstances, the actors nor the jargon—did this author repair in order to acquire the information he planned to pass on to his colleagues? It was

---

vexatious excesses from the other side."

I have only two comments to make. The first concerns my views on the vexed question of the relationship between church and state. "Mr Groen is now disposed to believe that the current situation has made a complete separation necessary in Holland. We may well suppose therefore that he is made up of two men, or rather two systems, which have not yet been harmonised." Let me reiterate: I have never proclaimed the union as an absolute and universal truth; I have long since demanded a genuine separation and emancipation of the Reformed Church, now regrettably subject to an arbitrary administration (see below, p. 32); Chalmers, the defender of union, was not inconsistent when he became founder of the Free Church of Scotland, nor was Mr de Rougemont when, having written that "the autonomy of the church did not imply its separation from the state," almost in the same breath maintained that "if the captivity of the church becomes slavery, the church will disappear from under the hand that crushes it, only to reappear free and independent." My second remark relates to our dear distinguished friend Mr da Costa, the recent loss of whom was nothing short of a national calamity for those who appreciated him. After Mr Trottet criticised our actions in 1842 and 1843 against the school in Groningen—actions by which, in his eyes, we powerfully contributed to support a waning reputation—he added: "However, the talented poet Mr da Costa, a converted Jew and lay theologian, chose his ground more wisely, and attacked the doctrines of this school from a religious perspective. But the kind of contempt with which the professional theologians greeted his criticism irritated his impressionable soul, and turned him away from any recognisable orthodoxy. And from that point on, we see him passionately striving to bring Judaism into Christianity, all the more unfortunate considering his immense influence." I repeat: I cannot blame Mr Trottet. He aspires to be a faithful reporter. But it puzzles me how those from whom it is reasonable to suppose he had gathered his information could have led him to write such lines on Mr da Costa's impressionable soul and recognisable orthodoxy as no one, apparently, would wish to endorse.

not difficult to discover. Clearly, he did not get his information from those he berates; neither from the orthodox nor the rationalists, neither from the ancient school of Dordt, nor from the schools of Groningen and Leyden. He could have repaired to no one but those in fact who in his estimation follow the current way of thinking, to our former brothers in arms, to those he specifies when he says: "I could cite distinguished laymen (allow me to add: *and pastors*) in that party, who, recognising at last that they had taken a wrong path, now resolved to take a more evangelical and enlightened one." As I pondered this significant passage, I felt that the affair was taking a far more serious turn and I decided, taking this article as my starting point, to explain from a much broader perspective a number of historical matters relating to our share of influence and responsibility in the events that then agitated (and still do agitate) the Dutch Reformed Church.

I gathered together what I had to say, in three chapters. The first was on the nature and aims of the *confessional party;* the second, on *the anti-revolutionary principle* in relation to the Gospel; and the last, on our *parliamentary opposition* from 1849 to 1857.

I would have liked to add (thinking of this essay as a kind of introduction) a more detailed and explanatory narrative of the different phases of the struggle we had to engage in to maintain Gospel truth in the church and in primary education. I do not know if I will be spared to undertake this task; but it seems to me that we have here already facts and reflections that support the theory encapsulated, in my opinion, in such a narrative. The real source of our weakness and disgrace, and the principal cause of the triumph of apathy and unbelief, lies in the influence of individualistic notions, which—sorry and strange mixture of Christianity and the ideas and spirit of the Revolution that they are—have a tendency to dissolve religious and political institutions and disrupt the course of the natural and historical life of society as a divine organism.

Before concluding this preface, I would like to pay homage to those of whom—on account of their merit, their talents, their steadfastness in difficult times—our party can rightly be proud. But their praise does not depend on me; such praise would be superfluous. Their names are inextricably bound up with the memory of our parliamentary and ecclesiastical struggles. And then again, it would be too painful for me, in mentioning them, to pass over in silence a multitude whose kindness and cooperation will never be erased from my memory, though they would care little now to be implicated by my homage, in any shape or form, in a misguided sense of responsibility.

It therefore remains for me to offer a few words of explanation—I might say interpretation—to curb, if possible, the hostility attached to the triple epithet: *anti-revolutionary, confessional, orthodox.*

We are the *Anti-Revolutionary Party*; that is to say, we are fighting the most fundamental errors in religion and politics; the teaching that replaces revealed truth and divine authority with the sovereignty of reason and the individual will, overthrows state and church and destroys the foundations of morality and society.

We are the *confessional* party; that is to say, we believe that every church should have a doctrine and be able to account for its hope and faith, and that the Dutch Reformed Church, once so illustrious and faithful, cannot proclaim unlimited freedom of doctrine, without denying its confession, its faith, and its history, and without breaking the bonds that link it to the Reformation of the sixteenth century and to the Holy Universal Church.

We are the *orthodox* party; that is to say, we profess the truths that the evangelical churches have expressed, with remarkable agreement, in their confessional statements: "the truths... by which one is a Christian, without which one is not; the truths of which the open profession, in word and deed, indicate to every Christian—and always will—a true brother in Christ; the truths of which not one could be excised without striking at the heart of Christianity."[5]

---

[5] Alexandre Vinet, *Liberté religieuse et questions ecclésiastiques* [Religious Liberty and Church Issues] (Paris: Chez les Éditeurs, Rue de Clichy 47, 1854), pp. 655–656.

Yes, for sure, we are the *orthodox confessional* party. Our first fundamental article is: Jesus Christ is our Saviour-God, who died for our sins and rose again for our justification; he is the Lamb of God who takes away the sin of the world.[6] There are, we believe, "some points of sound doctrine, knowledge of which is so necessary that no one should be ignorant of them or doubt them. They are the sure and indubitable principles and cardinal points of Christianity; as, for example, that there is one God; that Jesus Christ is the Son of God and God Himself; that our salvation rests solely on his mercy; and the like."[7] And just as every person must have a sense of his own continuity and identity, so, we say, should the church. "The church of the Apostles, the church of the Reformers, is in possession of the gospel of Jesus Christ, and has faithfully taught its doctrines. This is the legacy that has been handed down to us, and we cannot possibly ignore it. No doubt there may be new developments, but they always have their roots in the primary fundamental ideas. Progress in a building consists in erecting more and more on its foundations, not in knocking down its walls."[8] As far as we are concerned, without the doctrine of unmerited grace, which confesses Jesus Christ to be true man and true God, and accepts His death as a real atonement for sin, there can be no Reformed church and no Christian church.[9] As far as we are concerned, too, "the vision of Jesus Christ that gives us the courage to take up his cross and follow Him, is also the one that contemplates Him not as a mere role-model but as the only Saviour; not as a mere though extraordinary martyr, but as a divine victim; not only as the *Son of man* and truly man, but as the *Son of God* and truly God. This is the church that produced St John, St Paul, Luther, Calvin, Coligny, Wilberforce, every lowly and valiant soldier of Jesus Christ, and the martyrs of

---

[6] Martin Luther (provenance unknown).

[7] John Calvin, *Institutes of the Christian Religion,* Book III, ch. IV, sec. 1.

[8] Jean Henri Merle d'Aubigné (provenance unknown).

[9] Adolphus Monod (provenance unknown).

every age. To produce such Christians, we had need of such a Christ, and always will."[10]

What is the crucial issue we have with those who distance themselves from us, those whose disapproval ought the rather to have led them to know us better, when we use the word *confessional*? What, ultimately, is the issue behind their adverse comments? Is it that we are prone to be intolerant, that we have no regard for the rights of conscience, and that we endeavour to restrict freedom of the individual in matters of religion? The injustice of this oft-repeated accusation will be evident to all who take the trouble to read my apologetic publications. However the following preliminary remark will not be out of place: When we maintain that freedom of opinion *in the church* has its limits, our alleged intolerance is precisely what can be found in the two illustrious writers and advocates of freedom our opponents like to quote against us: Mr Vinet[11] and Mr Laboulaye.[12]

Mr Vinet wants freedom of worship and freedom of expression of religious beliefs; but he is as confessional as we are, if not more so. From a plethora of passages I have selected one at random: "When I say that orthodoxy cannot be established by authoritarian acts, I am not claiming that we must do nothing within the church to uphold sound doctrine. Rather, I believe that the notion of a confession of faith is inseparable from the notion of a church, and that the minister is bound to the confession of faith." Notice that Mr Vinet recommends the confession of faith and rule in the interests of freedom: "If we do not want to be bound by a confession of faith, we will have to

---

[10]P.-Tim. Larchevêque, *Revue Chrétienne, Recueil Mensuel,* Septième Année (Paris: Bureau de la Revue, 1860), pp. 318–319. Further details are lacking.

[11]Alexandre Vinet (1797–1847), Swiss Protestant theologian and literary critic, famed proponent of the strict separation of church and state.

[12] Édouard René de Laboulaye (1811–1883), French jurist, poet, and author, active in the anti-slavery movement.

take our chances with monopolies and steel ourselves against despotism.... Sooner or later, [we] have to come back to the true principles, [we] will have to have a confession of faith; and this rule will lead to freedom."[13]

Mr Laboulaye has written: "It is a crime to appeal to force, to oppress the soul that belongs to God and over which man has no rights. What is true of the individual is also true of the church; its only legitimate weapon is persuasion. To impose on me a creed that my faith rejects, to enforce silence on me, is to do me violence; basically, it is to deny human conscience, because conscience is the condition of being free to speak." Then, drawing a simple distinction that is constantly ignored by our detractors, Mr Laboulaye adds: "Is the church defenceless then? Certainly not; but its only jurisdiction is within its own realm; its authority extends only to the faithful who recognise its laws. There it is sovereign; there it commands; there it judges; there it has the right to excommunicate, that is to say, to exclude from its embrace any that do not accept the belief and rule it has established; there it has a duty to be intolerant and to root out infidelity."[14]

It may be that, in some circumstances, there are obstacles to the fulfilment of what Mr Laboulaye calls a duty. But what we should always disapprove in our friends' behaviour and changes of opinion is their abandoning the principle itself. They do not promote "the evangelical Protestant Reformed spirit; the traditional, historical, national, ecclesiastical spirit; the spirit that is faithful to the principles proclaimed by our fathers and the churches of the Reformation." They do not object to the "spirit that starts from an independent science, or from an absolute criticism, and that—forcing everything through the crucible of conscience or reason as the ultimate tribunal—ends in the assault on everything, the undermining of everything, and the dissolution of everything within sight." Notwithstanding their faith and

---

[13] Vinet, *Liberté religieuse et questions ecclésiastiques*, p. 134.

[14] *La liberté religieuse* (Paris: Charpentier, 1858), p. 6.

zeal for the advancement of the kingdom of God, it is by and large their fault that the evangelical current of thought undergirding the beliefs, faith and church of our fathers, is "in danger of losing itself in the arid desert sands of unbridled subjectivism, which belittles and undermines both Bible and Christ, and weakens and destroys both faith and church." [15]

The Hague,
June 1860

---

[15] *L'Espérance* of February 15th, 1860.

I. THE ORTHODOX CONFESSIONAL PARTY

The ultraorthodox circle in the Walloon community in The Hague

The following is Mr Trottet's description of the thinking of *ultraorthodox circles* in the Reformed Church in general and in the Walloon community in The Hague in particular.

> The spirit of the Canons of Dordt still drives the ultraorthodox circles in the church. Of such is the Walloon congregation in The Hague, which remains closed to any whiff of progress. It has increasingly cut itself off from the populace and deprived itself of the means of influencing it. So we end up with a closet piety, a schmaltzy Christianity, the fruit of a hothouse plant. This party — and it is a party — refuses to face the issues that confront it, preferring to remain undisturbed in its peaceful reverie, while it falls back on traditional dogma and creed rather than engage in life and faith. What is of importance, it appears, is the endless recitation of its *credo;* and it is not uncommon to witness the preference for an abrasive loveless orthodox person over a pious Christian whom gospel and conscience debar from subscribing to a narrow formula.

The picture is not flattering. But before I examine it, I think there are some issues of competence and propriety to be settled. Is a twelve-month residence sufficient for making such hard and fast decisions about such sensitive issues? Should he not have refrained from making a final assessment so soon? Should not prudence and charity, if not mere social convention — which the Christian is bound to respect in a gospel spirit — have cautioned this pastor against denouncing thus a whole section of the congregation before the Christian world? Did he have to treat these members of the flock as incorrigible? Could such an article ever be the means of restoring them to the fold? But I do not want to dwell on such things, persuaded as I am that Mr Trottet now regrets his hasty approach and is sensible of how much cause he had to write (to the editor of the magazine): "If I was adequately to respond to your request, I should, perhaps, have held back until I had had time to acquire a more thorough knowledge of the men and things about whom I have spoken to you."

Is this a true picture? I make no pretentions to drafting a panegyric of my friends; but by appealing to the good faith of those around me, I can happily issue a formal denial of these undoubtedly sincere but nonetheless thoughtless statements.

According to Mr Trottet, *a narrow formula*—the old orthodoxy of Dordt—is the idol and the creed of the circle he is attacking. A closer look should disabuse him in this matter, at the very least. This circle was not nurtured in the school of the Synod of Dordt, and it is not, to my knowledge, all that familiar with the writings of its doctors. It owes much to the gospel teaching and preaching of my excellent and worthy friend, Pastor Secrétan.[16] It has been fed on the writings of Newton[17] and Chalmers,[18] Rochat[19] and Gaussen,[20] Grand-Pierre[21] and Adolph Monod,[22] Merle d'Aubigné[23] and Vinet. It has been sustained

---

[16] J.C. Secrétan (1798–1875), Wallonian clergyman in The Hague, leader of the Réveil in the Netherlands.

[17] Dr J. Newton (1811–1891), American Presbyterian missionary to the Indies.

[18] Thomas Chalmers (1780–1847), Scottish preacher and political economist, leading light of the Church of Scotland.

[19] Auguste Louis Philippe Rochat (1789–1847), Swiss Protestant dissenting preacher and theologian.

[20] François Gaussen (1790–1863), Reformed clergyman at Geneva, leader of the Réveil, opponent of theological rationalism.

[21] Jean-Henri Grandpierre (1799–1870), Swiss clergyman and sponsor of missions.

[22] Adolphe Louis Frédéric Théodore Monod (1802–1856), French Protestant clergyman.

[23] Jean-Henri Merle d'Aubigné (1794–1872), Swiss Protestant clergyman and historian of the Reformation.

by the sermons—so full of unction and life—of Mr Kögel,[24] a distinguished student of Tholuck[25] and Neander,[26] and minister of the German congregation, which is certainly not ultrareformed. It admires our beautiful [Belgic] Confession of Faith, the Heidelberg Catechism, and many other admirable monuments of the living orthodoxy of a time when the scale of sacrifice testified to the sincerity of heart. It heartily confesses the leading doctrines proclaimed in the sixteenth century by the Protestant churches, and in the nineteenth by, for example, the Declaration of the Theological School of Geneva in 1831 and the Confession of the Free Church of the Canton of Vaud in 1846.

The deplorable influence of our extreme dogmatism is only too obvious to Mr Trottet; he recognises the bad tree by its paltry fruit. No progress, no life, no effect on its surroundings, no charity (especially no charity), no sympathy except for the "abrasive and loveless" orthodox who, with a naive boldness, exhibit no qualms in subscribing to formulas whose meaning and scope are beyond them. I want to draw a clear distinction here between a salutary warning and a somewhat acerbic criticism that seems undeserved to me. Ah! When it comes to paucity of life and charity, we certainly have more than enough reason to humble ourselves daily. We are far too involved in this lukewarmness, this easy Christianity, and all those weaknesses that characterise our time especially, and are doubly reprehensible in Christians. But there remains the question of whether Mr Trottet is entitled to point to the absence of Christian activity *as a distinctive feature* of the ultraorthodox circle, and as irrefutable proof of the shallowness of its life and faith? Only if, after a calm and impartial examination, he can

---

[24] Theodor Johannes Rudolf Kögel (1829–1896), founder and first pastor to the German Protestant congregation in The Hague.

[25] August Tholuck (1799–1877), German Protestant theologian, prominent member of the Evangelical Alliance.

[26] Johann August Wilhelm Neander (1789–1850), German Protestant theologian and church historian.

direct his shafts against it with a clear conscience, and can maintain that, in sad contrast with the rest of the flock, it gives no thought to the poor or popular education or any other Christian duty, either here or in neighbouring countries.

If indeed! Has Mr Trottet come across no one among those he labels ultraorthodox but the hard and splenetic, the rich in fine words and the poor in good works? Does every man among them shrink from engaging in the advancement of the kingdom of God? Are all their womenfolk indifferent to what does not concern their small circle of domestic interests, regarding the execution of their family tasks as the limit and fulfilment of their obligations? Such a summary of his experience is no small embarrassment to me. For it would be unbecoming to have to oppose this sorry picture with biographical revelations. I cannot set myself up as the panegyrist of my friends. I do not feel at liberty to put under the spotlight all those Christian women who have encouraged us and made us rejoice by what they have done for the relief of human misery. Happily, I may dare to believe that the ultraorthodox circle of the Walloon community in The Hague is not entirely unknown to our many co-religionists in France, Switzerland and, above all, Geneva and the canton of Vaud, and that the latter will put no implicit trust in Mr Trottet's impressions, which he has been far too hasty in recording.

Allow me one further observation: to fully comprehend a court injunction one has to see things from the judge's perspective. The *ultraorthodox* circle, he says. What can we say? The meaning of the adjective depends on Mr Trottet's own orthodoxy.

I keep my own counsel on the matter. But according to those whose opinion I value, his "orthodoxy" is rather vague and uncertain. Suffice it to transcribe here a few passages from the *Archives du Christianisme* [Archives of Christianity] and *Le Chrétien Évangélique du 19e siècle* [The Evangelical Christian in the Nineteenth Century] on the important work by Mr Trottet, published in 1856, *Les grands jours de l'Église apostolique* [The Great Times of the Apostolic Church]. It is a carefully written book, the fruit of considerable meditation, "a work of conviction, one that I have long carried in my heart," to quote his own words.

In the *Archives* for 30 August 1859, Pastor Pozzy[27] wrote: "It would be very difficult to respond to what Mr Trottet asks us to believe regarding man's fallen state and his redemption, the two poles of the evangelical system. We must even confess that from our point of view there are pages that have saddened us; not that the truth has been attacked, either directly or indirectly, but it is certainly misunderstood." And, despite a letter of six large quarto pages in which Mr Trottet set out to refute this assessment of him, on the 30 September Frédéric Monod[28] wrote: "For the time being, we do no more than stand by Mr Pozzy's article... It is open to everyone to read the book in question, to read Mr Pozzy's wholly respectful, well-meaning and serious criticism, and to judge for himself whether this criticism is as unfounded as the author maintains." In *Le Chrétien Évangélique* Mr J. Panchaud[29] is just as negative: "Sin, the sense of sin, pardon in Christ and by faith in this pardon, the gift of eternal life, which is the source of love in the spirit—herein is the genesis of the new creature; on these issues we would have liked to see more emphasis placed in a work that is eager to inculcate charity." Then, addressing the issue of the expiatory value of the Lord's death, he adds, "The page that ought to have been the crucial page seems very weak and pale to us. While, through events and in Scripture, God has clearly spoken *in a manner intended to be understood*, Mr. Trottet has not spoken so as to be understood by any of his readers who are still strangers to the Gospel. Neither has he done so in a manner that will satisfy Christians of the *old school;* rather I fear he has satisfied those who oppose evangelical orthodoxy. In any case, while this page does not allow me to infer the author's

---

[27]Benjamin Pozzy (1820–1905), Swiss Protestant pastor of republican leanings.

[28]French Protestant pastor and brother of Adolphe Monod.

[29]Jean Panchaud (dates unknown), Swiss Protestant clergyman.

doctrine, I must nevertheless inform him that one could draw conclusions from the lacunae of this work, and from this one in particular, that would be quite severe."

It is not I who insist on drawing attention to these lacunae, or who draws conclusions from them with a severity that, in my view and with my limited information, may be misplaced; far from it, I would rather believe, until it is proven otherwise, that deep down Mr Trottet and I agree far more than he might suppose. The net result of these observations is that he does not always speak with accuracy and clarity; that his sermons have imposed on his hearers the duty of guarding against misunderstanding (a duty that can assume the appearance of a lack of trust in his fidelity, says Mr Panchaud); that a degree of embarrassment and coldness must inevitably arise between him and the ultraorthodox circle. And finally, it was therefore doubly necessary for him to be wary of his first impressions, and to pass on nothing of them until they had matured under a more thoughtful reflection. While we would have liked to elicit from him an understanding of the essential doctrines of the Gospel more in keeping with the legitimate desires of old school Christians, we shall nevertheless have little cause for being upset by his aspersions of our being, in his opinion, *ultraorthodox;* that is, more orthodox than himself.

My portrait

Mr Trottet has taken the liberty of attaching a portrait of me to his description of the ultraorthodox party.

> This party has a man of outstanding character and talent in Mr Groen van Prinsterer, a former member of the States General. A mind enamoured of the past, he has attached himself with a measure of pig-headedness to the ecclesiastical system represented by Stahl and Hengstenberg in Germany, though with modifications in keeping with the Reformed Church. So we can think of him as the Stahl of Holland. His prejudice is clear; he appears to have read

I. The Orthodox Confessional Party

books by the opposite camp only to uncover their blind spots. This is certainly not the way to make real progress; and it is very likely that if this ardent opponent of the separation of church and state had been born in the Anglican Church, his principle would have led him along a logical path to Puseyism. His unswerving loyalty to this principle and his strength of character have had, in many respects, a good influence. But they have nevertheless contributed to the isolation of the orthodox party; and his refusal, on his own account as well as others', to examine everything with a view to extracting what is good, has increasingly operated to limit his personal influence.

It is not for me to judge the accuracy, or challenge the propriety, of these psychological observations. If I have indeed not read the works of my opponents other than to discover the chink in their armour, Mr Trottet is right: "This is not the way to make real progress." If I refuse to submit to careful scrutiny, he may furthermore conclude, quite reasonably, that such unreasonable pig-headedness will soon leave me all alone on my error-strewn path. I can only say that I have not acted so intentionally. My desire has been, in the interest of debate, to do full justice to my antagonists; I have tried to practise a Christian eclecticism, the touchstone of which is God's Word.

But while one should remain silent about assertions like this, I do not believe one should refuse to explain one's principles.

I *am* enamoured of the past. For sure I am. I do not believe it possible to break with the past. I believe that every notion connected with the future is rooted in the past.

I *am* stubborn in my defence of the ecclesiastical system represented in Prussia by distinguished men whom some regard as having a strong inclination towards Puseyism. So what? Is Mr Trottet referring to the maintenance of doctrine? Then it is useless going all the way to Germany; in France and Switzerland he will find more than enough published names with whom I am in agreement on this matter. Or is it the church organisation he had in mind? I think I am, in that matter at least, for those who know me, free from suspicion. I have consistently opposed the hierarchical system imposed on our church since 1816; no one has been a greater advocate of the rights of the congregation, of the equality of pastors, of the influence of the laity, or of the universal priesthood. "The church," said Vinet, "is the believers; the church must govern itself; the preachers of the gospel are not the only ministers; there is, technically speaking, no *clergy* in an evangelical church: the whole church is the clergy, the Lord's inheritance, Jesus Christ's patrimony." These are Presbyterian maxims; they are what I profess; clearly, I run less risk of becoming Puseyite than of becoming puritanical.

I *am* an ardent opponent of the separation of church and state; though not as ardent as Mr Trottet imagines. One could also speak of Mr Vinet as an ardent proponent of it. I count myself among his most sincere admirers; but by advocating an absolute separation, as a universal truth, and thus raising it to the rank of an article of faith, I have to concede that he has made a serious mistake. For, there have been times when, in the interests of religious freedom, the exercise of political rights had to be restricted to members of the State Church. In the times of St Bartholomew,[30] or the League,[31] or the Thirty-Years War, or the Revocation of the Edict of Nantes,[32] or the atrocious persecution of the field conventicles,[33] or when wars of religion and conquest were intertwined, would it have been at all safe to advocate an absolute equality for all in Protestant states, and to rely on the scrupulous honesty and good graces of the duly grateful Catholics? Or in England in

---

[30] A reference to the St Bartholomew's Day Massacre of August 1572, when thousands of French Protestants were slaughtered by Catholics.

[31] The Catholic League, formed in 1576 to eradicate Protestantism from France.

[32] The Edict of Nantes (1598) granted toleration to French Protestants. It was revoked in 1685 by Louis XIV.

[33] A reference to the "Desert" period from the Revocation of the Edict of Nantes to the French Revolution, in which the French Protestant churches met clandestinely amidst persecution.

the glorious year of 1688, was William III mistaken when, called upon to lay the foundations of a genuine liberty, he refused to be taken in by the Stuarts' ardour for toleration? Force of circumstance has in the past made the union of church and state necessary and advantageous, and may yet do so again in the future. The first principle of ecclesiastical law is not separation but *independence*. "Insist on independence," said Mr Gasparin[34] many years ago, "not on separation. Independence is a dogma inscribed on every page of the Bible; separation is nowhere written therein." It is the church's duty, everywhere and at all times, to maintain the independence of the spiritual order. When it is faithful in this duty, the benefits of union can be appreciated and, if and when necessary, it will be abandoned (while retaining the principle) in the interests of truth. We have seen instances of this in Scotland and in the canton of Vaud. Dr Chalmers is a proponent of union but also the founder of the Free Church of Scotland. Without denying the rule, he has justified the exception by his own example. It would be a great mistake to suppose that I am currently advocating what Mr Trottet means by union. Under no circumstances am I aiming for the restoration of a privileged church. In my estimation, political equality irrespective of religious views is progress. In the current situation and in the light of prevailing ideas, I believe that there would be serious difficulties with what's left of the old order, without what union used to bring to it. For the Reformed Church in particular, I have long sought genuine separation, that is, the emancipation of a church from its miserable subjection to arbitrary administrative power. No more caesaropapism, no more *jus in sacra*, especially no more civil religion; nothing but a right to supervise and duty to protect.

With Mr Guizot,[35] I want "a separation of the spiritual and temporal orders. In varying degrees of articulation and development, one

---

[34] Agénor Étienne, Comte de Gasparin (1810–1871), French statesman and author.
[35] François Pierre Guillaume Guizot (1787–1874), French statesman and historian, of old Calvinistic stock.

of the characteristic—perhaps the most characteristic—feature of modern societies is just this: The separation of the religious and civil orders, and the outlawing of all forcible intervention in the spiritual order, even in the interests of truth." But also with him, and in the sense he intended, I might add: "not the separation of church and state, a blunt instrument that degrades and weakens the one as much as the other, under the pretext of freeing them from each other."[36] What I want is a secular or lay state, but one still Christian, not a state that refuses to recognise divine authority, with church and state as distinct entities acting—each in its own sphere and in concert—for the advancement of the nation's best interests. Is this too much to ask? Do you really think the idea of a Christian state is a pipe-dream? Ah well, at least grant me the existence of a natural and indissoluble union between a people and its beliefs; therein is reason enough for the state to adapt its laws and institutions to the nation's religious interests and needs. The governments of Europe need to remember that they rule over *Christian* peoples. Such a union, the only one—in my opinion—on which we should not turn our backs, is subject to a number of conditions, I believe; conditions of the highest value in Vinet's estimation: a clear separation between the categories of *believer* and *citizen*, the autonomy and sovereignty of every church in the whole range of its essential and legitimate rights, and respect for individual conscience in its practical manifestations.

---

[36]This quotation is a conflation of citations from two separate works: "La Belgique et le roi Léopold en 1857," *Revue des Deux Mondes,* 2e, tome 10, 1857, p. 493, and *De la démocratie en France* [Regarding Democracy in France] (Paris: Victor Masson, 1849), pp. xxi-xxii.

I. The Orthodox Confessional Party

Mr Trottet has compared my opinions, in some respects, to those of Hengstenberg[37] and Stahl,[38] two great names that fill me with admiration. At a time when one quite literally needed to have the courage of one's convictions, the *Evangelische Kirchen-Zeitung* [Evangelical Church Gazette] in Berlin rendered invaluable service to the cause of the Gospel. I do not know anyone who has equalled Mr Stahl in the scientific demonstration of the fact that revealed truth is the first and indispensable condition of freedom and progress. Being called "the Stahl of Holland" would be doing me too much honour, if I did not know that, in the mouths of those who proclaim it, it is not at all meant as a compliment. I know too that as a result of wilful prejudice this name has become a veritable bugaboo for many of our friends in Switzerland and France. And I know that once we are linked with Hengstenberg and Stahl we are doomed: we judge and anathematise, we belong to the most reactionary and intolerant party, and we think we are authorised to treat people with disdain, and indulge in a slighting and cavalier criticism; all to the inevitable astonishment of posterity. There is a good example of this in the issue of *Le Chrétien Évangélique* [The Evangelical Christian] that contains Mr Trottet's article. Mr Stahl had not long before published something on the Lutheran Church and Union. It was admired even by antagonists like Nitzsch[39] and Hoffmann[40] and by other theological luminaries in Germany. *Le Chrétien Évangélique* did not share their opinion. It cast his book aside with a flick of its pen: "Prussian Puseyism has exploded in this book by the famous Dr Stahl, a work of no scientific or theological value." Poor

---

[37] Ernst Wilhelm Hengstenberg (1802–1869), German Lutheran churchman and professor of theology in Berlin, defender of the divine character of the Bible.

[38] Friedrich Julius Stahl (1802–1861), German Lutheran professor of constitutional law in Berlin, stalwart defender of the Christian state.

[39] Apparently Karl Immanuel Nitzsch (1787–1868), German Lutheran theologian.

[40] Apparently Ludwig Friedrich Wilhelm Hoffmann (1806–1873), German Lutheran theologian, a member of King Friedrich Wilhelm IV's inner circle.

Mr Stahl! Who will want to cast an eye over his works now, knowing they are so worthless! Still, one writer whose judgement does have some value—Mr Vinet—spoke in a much less cavalier fashion when, in his *Essay ... Upon the Separation of Church and State* (see note on p. 123 below), he put some substance into his critical remarks. In the second edition, he repeats the criticism but adds: "We have studied Mr Stahl's observations with respectful attention."

The confessional party in the Reformed Church

If Mr Trottet is to be believed, unbelief should now make rapid progress in the Netherlands. There is nothing to resist it since, as he says, all we have is this lifeless and loveless circle, devoid of living faith; a circle that has nothing but its formulas with which to support and rally the cause; a circle made up of yesterday's men; the ultraorthodox circle. Three major theological currents, he says, are disputing the field; the school of Groningen, which has no clearly defined principles and sees in Christ only an exceptional teacher; the school of Leyden, which has replaced the Gospel with a new formula of its own and has no room for what is called sin. And the third current, which has taken its stand against the other two...? Is it the party of the truth in its many shades? No, it is nothing more than the old orthodoxy of Dordt. On the one hand, he says, we have rationalism and all that goes with it; on the other hand, we have a dead faith and traditional dogma. This is a very inaccurate picture. It entirely ignores the origin, nature, strengths and diversity of the evangelical party. It entirely ignores the *Réveil*. It entirely ignores the fact that in Holland and elsewhere, since 1813 and 1815, after the horrors of revolution and war and the blessings of deliverance, and especially since the upheavals of 1830, the life-giving breath of the Holy Spirit has given birth to a genuine Christianity. Being thus brought to the knowledge of the Gospel, we formed a bond, founded on the great biblical facts, with a considerable body of people who were already in the Reformed Church, and who had preserved—with varying degrees of fidelity and life—the precious deposit of faith; however, in and of itself, the Réveil was neither Calvinist, Lutheran nor Mennonite; it was *Christian*. The Réveil did not look to the old orthodoxy of Dordt as its standard but to that of the Reformation: the Word of God. And while it was happy enough to discover the doctrine of salvation admirably expressed in our creeds and set high store by a body of teaching so conformable to Holy Scripture; and while, too, it was opposed to the infiltration of rationalism into the church's doctrine and the clergy's duties, it hardly dreamed of embracing or imposing these formulas on anyone as an absolute and literal rule with an absurd and childish obsessiveness. A spirit of Christian brotherhood prevailed over any such tendencies. Most distinguished men gave it their blessing. They accommodated their enthusiasm for sound doctrine to a sincere desire not to hinder fraternal union by attaching undue weight to minor differences, real or imagined.

Permit me to draw your attention to one of them, one who was a model of this generous spirit and whose name is close to my heart: Mr de Clercq.[41] He will never be forgotten in Geneva; in him the most simple and sincere faith was united with the finest gifts of taste and intelligence. I might also mention an outstanding poet, the celebrated Bilderdijk,[42] who, by the breadth of his talent and work, and even more by the forcefulness of his character, has had so great an influence on contemporary youth. And while his utterances were sometimes a little too colourful, he never forgot that the purpose and goal of a Christian exclusiveness is to safeguard the foundations of the truth that all genuine believers have in common. Moreover, in offering the hand of friendship to the zealous sectaries of Dordt, his disciples generally followed their Master's example; whatever there was of hardness in the

---

[41] Willem le Clercq (1795–1844), Dutch businessman and supporter of the Réveil movement.

[42] Willem Bilderdijk (1756–1831), Dutch poet and proponent of royalist conservatism.

manner in which his genius expressed itself was often softened under the impulses of charity. The most illustrious representative of his school, my friend da Costa,[43] has deservedly had a profound influence on many Christians. He has persistently rejected everything that would try or tend to interpose any kind of authority between man's conscience and God's Word. Finally, Mr Trottet's mistake—that of trying to squeeze all the orthodox into the narrow confines of the very precise and abstract formulas of the 1619 Synod—presents us (nowadays especially) with a bizarre contrast to the very real trend that looks like becoming universal, even among Christians, and that is increasingly moving towards an *individualism* of absolute freedom in all its manifestations, and with no concern for the Reformed Church or the historical unity of its faith.

No doubt in many of our Reformed churches there have been, and still are, circles of varying proportions—against whom the charge of dead orthodoxy is occasionally but not generally warranted—who are tempted to make scrupulous fidelity to the anti-Remonstrant formula the necessary and defining mark of a Christian. But this group, which has considerable support among the working classes, has not only had no marked influence on public life, but has often been swayed by our wishes and advice. As a result, it has renounced an untimely dogmatism on more than one occasion. And the misconceived notion of making the Canons of Dordt the touchstone of our day—something Mr Trottet thinks is our overriding obsession—has met with stiff opposition among us.

What! (they protest) aren't you supposed to be at the head of the *confessional* and *legal* party? You have approved, shared in, and fanned this passion for creed and dogma. You have advocated the nor-

---

[43]Isaac da Costa (1798–1860), Dutch poet, protégé of Bilderdijk, and Jewish convert to Christianity.

mative authority of the Reformed confession; you have said—and repeated it a hundred times—that every member of the church must strive to uphold its doctrine.

For a long time now, either through wilful or unintentional misunderstanding, they have trotted out these assertions, and condemned us. Yes, indeed, there has been a distinct *confessional* party, advocating the right and duty of the church to maintain her faith; a party that has on occasions called me, by a combination of circumstances and in difficult times, to be its mouthpiece. But the charge of reckless and passionate exaggeration will vanish—I make so bold as to affirm it—at least in the eyes of most people, once they are prepared to consider things from our perspective. This is a matter for explanation, not incrimination.

I belong to a church that is second to none in the magnificence of its origin, in the splendour of its struggles, in the light of its devout teachers, in the devotion of its martyrs, and in the purity of its faith. I belong to a church *national* in its numbers, its influence, and its memorials. When we saw it under attack from unbelief, we could see no other course but that of not slighting the advantages of the current situation, of not abandoning the fundamentals and continuity of its traditional and historical faith, of not forgetting that every member of the church—lay and clerical—is bound to defend its beliefs and its autonomy, and so ensure the nation—formed and reformed by the Good News—the priceless privileges of a Christian people.

Its principles with respect to the creeds

Nothing excessive, nothing extraordinary: our system is none other than what has always been considered inseparable from the very notion of a church. There has to be some agreement, among those who meet together, to form the base of a common worship. It is the most elementary and modest of systems; it is what is nowadays constantly advocated by Christians who could never be suspected of intolerance, in particular by Adolphe Monod, in his essays *l'Exclusivisme* [Exclusivism] and *Pourquoi je demeure dans l'Eglise établie* [Why I Remain in the Established Church], and by Vinet (as can be seen in the anthology *Liberté religieuse et questions ecclésiastiques* [Religious Liberty and the Church Question]) at every stage of his career.

We shall note here, in just a few words, our principle, its scope, its necessity, and its practical consequences.

The principle is inseparable from the idea of a common worship. Every church has its doctrine; herein lies its character, its life, its essence, and the moral bond that forms the reality and unity of the ecclesiastical body. This doctrine is well known; it appears in its history, it is contained in its creeds, its liturgy, and its confession of faith, which is the system of teaching freely accepted by the express or implied adherence of its members. A confession is indispensable; it exists even before it is formally drafted: "Assume for the sake of argument that there is a church with nothing resembling a confession of faith. If there was a serious division in its ranks, it would be forced to *put its customs in writing*."[44] "When its confession of faith is expunged, the church can no longer be found."[45]

Now what is the scope of this principle, and in what sense have we advocated its application? We have not assigned any inherent power to the confession, either active or independent; but we have resisted its tacit repeal, and we have insisted on its continuing value as a defensive treaty of alliance, as a rallying point, as a useful research tool, and as an invaluable work of reference.[46] Maintaining the great truths of Christianity—the truths of the Gospel and the Reformation—has been our starting point; to these truths we have given an exclusive right of citizenship in the church, and by resting our case on the confession and other witnesses to our common faith, we have appealed to the

---

[44]Vinet, *Liberté religieuse et questions ecclésiastiques*, p. 212.

[45]*Ibid.*, p. 217.

[46]*Ibid.*, p. 206.

I. The Orthodox Confessional Party

conscience, and even to the loyalty, of our opponents, against an unbridled subjectivism that would destroy the church in order to preserve the shadow and the form.

The necessity of such an appeal is evident. Otherwise the church would disappear, or at least no longer deserve the name.

The Bible, we are told, is sufficient. "The Bible, which has been invoked by parties that accuse each other of being unbiblical, cannot possibly serve as a confession for anyone."[47] "Invoking it to settle controversies would only serve to start up new ones. It would simply set every variant of the faith at loggerheads, and most variants of unbelief as well."[48]

Should we really be concerned, they say, about abolishing a document that is rarely referred to, exercises little influence, and is almost forgotten? "It is all too clear that we only think about abolishing it because its influence *is* felt and it has become a nuisance: we do not attack the dead, we leave the dying to die."[49]

Take from the church every doctrine that unites and by the same token excludes, advocate the freedom and equality of all opinions, destroy the confession; and what will become of the church? It will no longer exist; religion will become no more than a department of state.[50] You will see the state trying to build cohesion into a dysfunctional church that is falling apart on all sides, trying to replace the lack of unity in doctrine with an administrative office.[51]

Church folk will be prey to every wind of doctrine. There is no guarantee that the Gospel will be proclaimed to them. Where remains the freedom of parishes, where the freedom of the believer, if, instead

---

[47] *Ibid.*, p. 211.

[48] *Ibid.*, p. 225.

[49] *Ibid.*, p. 213.

[50] *Ibid.*, p. 219.

[51] *Ibid.*, p. 220.

of confessional men for pastors, they are obliged to endure men of the prevailing opinion?[52]

But there's more. When we exclude *no* opinion, by the same token we exclude every *exclusive* opinion; the truth, the Gospel, has no place in this syncretism. Tolerance of erroneous opinions can only be provisional or exceptional; for where error is allowed free rein, truth becomes a seed of confusion, and can only be accommodated by denying its nature and obligations and leaving error in peace.

There are practical consequences that flow from these essential, natural relations between a church and its doctrine.

We must remain in the church. "The orthodox faith is, whatever people may say, the one faith of our church. It is an indisputable fact.... The evangelical doctrine lies at the foundation of our church; it is its legal, historical and *de facto* doctrine; in short, the church has every title to it, while heterodoxy and latitudinarianism have none. Therefore, we can and do say: We are at home here; it is not up to us to take ourselves off somewhere else, we will only leave when we are hounded out."[53] We must remain here so that, when we are hounded out, we will leave with our honour intact and a real victory snatched from the jaws of seeming defeat. We must remain here until we have drawn attention to the real issues, until we have warned and informed the masses, until we have built up the existing church and so prepared one of those joint exoduses that, as Mr de Gasparin used to say, carry off the institution and its standards.

We must remain in the church, in order to fight for it. We must fight determinedly and sternly, not mindlessly or rashly; we must be uncompromising and relentless, until the goal is reached and the church has triumphed, either by being set back on its unalterable foundations or, overpowered by force and injustice, by re-forming—free,

---

[52]*Ibid.*, p. 225.

[53]Monod, *Pourquoi je demeure dans l'Église établie*, pp. 30, 28.

independent, and with renewed vigour. "One of two things must happen: either the organisation is gently but irresistibly brought back to life and conformed to the course and exigencies of life; or, if the evil is incurable, it will become impossible to stay in the church and we will have to leave. For, victorious or crestfallen, that is the glorious alternative of Christian life within the visible church."[54]

Such was our *legal* point of view; at the same time, it was our *moral* point of view.

There is nothing as immoral as divorcing law from morality.

There is nothing as immoral as the deliberate substitution of the church's faith with opinions that subvert it.

There is nothing as immoral as the abuse of powers confided by the church, and arming oneself with them against it, with the intent to war against it in all that is most fundamental.

You will retort: You could always be mean and childish and insist on your indisputable rights: *summum jus, summa injuria* [the height of justice is the height of injustice]. No doubt we could, but in this instance at least, the adage is not needed. Our motto has always been: *in necessariis unitas, in dubiis libertas, in omnibus caritas* [In things necessary, unity; in things doubtful, liberty; in everything, charity]. In keeping with the evangelical spirit, we have adopted this motto wholeheartedly. So there are *necessary* truths; truths with which any meddling is unlawful; truths the detractors of which the church cannot tolerate or embrace without abandoning its faith.

But has this inerrant system actually erred in practice? Were our demands, for what we regard as fundamental truths, really about articles of indifferent theological or religious consequence that may, with a little prodding, become the source of doubt and controversy in the church?

Quite the contrary. Wherever there has been a Christian revival—we mean in our time, not centuries ago—we have always restricted

---

[54]*Ibid.*, p.44.

ourselves to what is considered the *minimum* for evangelical unity. When I look back over our long string of declarations, I can summarise them all in the Confession already referred to: the popular Confession that was adopted unanimously in 1846 as the expression of dogmatic unity in the Church of the canton of Vaud.

> The Free Church is connected through the unity of its faith to the apostolic church and to churches of all times that have professed the doctrine of free salvation through the blood of Christ. It is therefore joined to the evangelical churches of the sixteenth century, who expressed their faith with such remarkable agreement in their confessional statements, especially in the Helvetic Confession of Faith. Together with them, it proclaims the divine inspiration, the authority and the complete sufficiency of the Holy Scriptures of the Old and New Testaments. It professes its faith in one God—Father, Son and Holy Spirit. It acknowledges man's fallen state, his sin and consequent condemnation; that there is only one means for his salvation, namely living faith in Jesus Christ, God manifest in the flesh, true God and true man, the only Mediator between God and man, and high priest of the New Covenant; that he died for our sins and rose again for our justification; that he ascended to the right hand of God, and possesses all power on earth and in heaven, from where he communicates to believers and the church, through the Holy Spirit sent from his Father, every grace necessary for regeneration and good works, and from whence he will return to raise the dead, to judge the world with justice and confer eternal life on his people. In short, he has power to save to the uttermost all who come to God through him. This, the church holds, is the heart and foundation of Christian truth.

It must demand, then, in the church's name—by an appeal to its confession and history—resistance to the systematic undermining of these central truths, and rally the faithful around the foundations of its faith; at the same time, we believe, it must oppose the machinations of the ultraorthodox, and take account of the needs and circumstances of the time. This is what the confessional party set out to do. Let us see whether or not it has diverged from this path.

The orthodoxy of Dordt

Before we begin, let's look at the nature and limits of our practical commitment to the old orthodoxy of Dordt. It has been a constant refrain that we want to reintroduce it and impose it by force; that this has always been our real if unspoken goal; and that we see adherence to the Standards of 1619 as the only way to defeat modern errors. Let us see whether this is so, and whether, in the current struggles, we have had recourse to these seventeenth-century weapons.

I am not going to discuss the political question. I have attempted to deal with it impartially elsewhere. I have recognised Oldenbarnevelt's talents and services, been open about Prince Maurice's flaws, and kept in mind that the history of their antagonism and the fatal discussions in the Republic have been highly distorted by the virulence of prejudice and memory. Many long-held opinions have now had to give way before new evidence, based on advances in historical research and the testimony of previously-unknown documents. Those who have seriously studied the question will not find either inaccurate or overly harsh what I already dared to say in 1841: "It is now clear that most of the States of Holland, guided by Oldenbarnevelt, exercised a monopoly of power without check or limit in the interests of the aristocratic community; and that they persecuted the orthodox Reformed, fined them, threw them into prison, and deprived them of their civil and commercial rights. These *protectors of civil liberty* even forbade recourse to the law and held the army in their pay, so that they could maintain their absolutism against all and everyone. In short, despite the States General and the Stadtholder, they played fast and loose with the citizenry and violated their most sacred rights." In the Republic of the United Provinces things had come to such a pretty pass that the only choice lay between suppression of these excesses and civil war.

I shall also pass by the ecclesiastical question. Only recall, in passing, that the independence of the church had been almost destroyed; that the magistrates—on the advice of a relatively small number of pastors who could only be maintained in the Reformed Church by the secular arm—believed themselves authorised to conclude that doctrines anathema to the church would be tolerated without contradiction, and that therefore they need have no qualms about imposing their sovereign good pleasure on the church in religious matters; that they rejected the only legitimate means of decision-making, namely the convening of a national synod; that they then turned down any amicable arrangement that would give each party its own churches; and that, finally, when the Reformed yielded to force and abandoned the Reformed churches to the Arminians, taking refuge in barns and in private houses, they denied them even this last moiety of freedom.

Let us return to the crucial issue: the theology of Dordt.

Generally speaking, the theology of Dordt is neither more nor less than the theology of the Reformation. The latter was the theology of our forefathers, formed in the light of the Gospel and the glow of martyrs' pyres. It was based on Holy Scripture as being the only rule of faith; and after a renewed examination of the liturgical Confession, the Synod saw no need to make any changes of theological significance.

The special work of this Synod was to come up with a reasoned interpretation of the point at issue, *the doctrine of predestination*. That's no big surprise, you will say, but what is your own opinion? Do you approve of these famous Canons? In your opinion, was the Synod's task necessary and beneficial, and if so, do you intend to include it as a binding rule in the Reformed Church you want to rejuvenate?

To these two questions—*Do you agree?* and *Do you follow the same line?*—there cannot be a single answer. When we recall that the reason behind resistance to the Arminian subtleties was to defend the central truth of the gospel, free salvation, we will see that if we try to do today what was then praiseworthy, we will make a huge mistake and engage in a pitiful anachronism.

Yes, certainly, by insisting on the doctrine of election, formulated with exacting precision, our seventeenth century forefathers were absolutely right. Why? Because at that time to deny election was the first link in a chain of logical deduction that would end in conditional salvation.

Here I must take a back seat in order to introduce some witnesses in support of my thesis, witnesses no one will challenge.

In 1620, the French Churches, which adhered to the Synod of Dordt (it is often forgotten that it was an ecumenical Synod of Reformed churches), expressed themselves thus: "I condemn the doctrine of the Arminians, because it makes the election of believers dependent on man's will and hence attributes so much power to his free will as to destroy the grace of God; and because it is disguised popery intent on insinuating Pelagianism among us, and hence undermining all certainty with regard to salvation."[55]

That is as plain as plain can be. Now listen to what Merle d'Aubigné had to say two centuries later: "When was the Church of Holland triumphant and glorious? When she marched at the head of all the churches of Christendom? No, but when it was given her, within the walls of Dordt, to bear the most complete, the most magnificent witness that it has ever been vouchsafed man to bear, to the grace of Jesus Christ."

So we are fully justified, in my estimation, in attributing some worth to the old orthodoxy of Dordt, even in what was uniquely characteristic of it.

The dean of the Lausanne and Vevay presbytery[56] thought so too, as he made clear when he wrote to our synodical commission in 1837: "The purer the doctrine, the holier the life, the more the church will

---

[55] Part of the oath required by the Synod of Alez, 1620.

[56] V. Melley, Swiss Protestant clergyman (further details are lacking).

flourish. If God has reserved for yours such glorious times as those of illustrious memory, when the eyes of Reformed Europe were on it, it will be by firmly embracing this doctrine of grace that God has charged it to defend, and which it has indeed already explained and defended in a famous assembly with a fidelity that has earned it the recognition of all evangelical churches, and especially ours. The free election of God is the crown of a believer's faith, as it is of Christian theology."[57]

But if this is so, how can we endorse such praise and not be imitators of those who earn it? Can we praise the Synod's work so highly and yet refrain from making the decisions of Dordt a mandatory rule for all time?

We can and we must. While fully approving the inflexibility of our forefathers, we must beware of blindly following their example. We must act differently, though for the same reason.

A truth that was once the focus of evangelical struggle can become an entirely secondary matter, as circumstances link it with, or separate it from, what is fundamental in the Gospel. At the time there was a real danger from the link between the Arminian errors and those of Pelagianism and Socinianism; nowadays, however, the doctrine of predestination is often misunderstood; the Canons of Dordt especially (though generally speaking hardly known) come up against fierce opposition among the most respectable Christians. The very formula that then guarded against a false brotherhood would now be an obstacle to a genuine one. How then should we sensibly imitate our forefathers? By following the wise counsel of the dean of Lausanne; by embracing the doctrine of grace more firmly than ever, but without digging ourselves in behind a barricade the quality and scale of which bear no relation to the nature of the assault; by not trying to extend the controversy beyond the critical issue; by not looking for the confession of our unity in an abstruse and impenetrable doctrine, which the

---

[57] *Archives du christianisme*, 20e année, 2e série 5 (1837), p. 154.

theologians of Dordt themselves admitted should be maintained only with extreme caution, as it is beyond the comprehension of the common man and can be easily misunderstood and gravely distorted.

That is why we are opposed to any public outcry in support of this theological formula. For example, at a well-publicised reunion of the Friends of the Church in the Amsterdam Assembly of 1848, the discussion turned to a consideration of this issue. As president, I hastened to warn them of the dangers of an undue and untimely fidelity. There is no question, I said, of denying the doctrine or of erasing it from our confessional standards; but what is required is that we be attentive to the realities of the current situation. When we appeal to the doctrines of our church in order to weed out those who undermine its evangelical foundations, we should never provoke a fatal split between those we are trying to unite (and who sincerely want to join forces on the essential verities of our common faith) by lumping together essential truths and things on which Christians are divided. This was not a clever tactic on my part just to get a feigned agreement, but an attitude perfectly consistent with the goal we aimed at and the principles we had laid down.

Our attitude towards dissent, rationalism in the church, the theological faculties, and primary education

But have we always used this language? Have we displayed the same broadness of mind, the same opposition to an unreasonably strict orthodoxy in all our endeavours? Have we never been tempted to insist on the antiquated formulas and dogmatic teachings of an over-the-top Calvinism?

In order to show that our conduct has been consistently dictated by the same spirit, I want to look at the four principal issues on which we focussed our attention between 1837 and 1848. They were the liberty of dissenters, the unity of doctrine, the teaching of the theological faculties, and primary education. At every point we fell back on the church's law, its doctrine, and its confession of faith. We never overstepped the boundaries of our system; we restricted ourselves, even in the Reformed Church, to the defence of interests common to all Christians.

In 1837 when, for the first time, I found myself called upon to fight in the arena of ecclesiastical rights, the issue facing us was the freedom of worship of Reformed dissenters. The evangelical fervour of the Réveil on the one hand, and the infidelity or indifference of ministers on the other, had led to an explosion of dissent. With a hunger and a thirst for sermons consistent with the Word of God, many ordinary believers either rashly set up separate churches under the guidance of a number of young ministers or sought edification in conventicles without going to quite such extremes. Indignant at this disorderly presumption, the ecclesiastical authorities made no effort to trace out the causes but hastily set out to stifle the seeds of disunion and division. The rebel ministers had to be recalled to their duty, and the lost sheep returned to their fold; the prospects of independence were intolerable. Fortunately, it was said, the existing laws provided a very effective means of maintaining unity. The Synod, which was little more than an administrative office for the civil authorities, and which inspired no confidence and had no moral influence, was not ashamed to ask the government for support and to insist on the strict application of clauses that the suspicious despotism of Bonaparte had added to the Penal Code.

The state was cajoled in this despicable manner. It dispersed the meetings with armed force. It hauled the separatists, and especially their pastors, before the courts. It fined and imprisoned them. The most despicable means were used to overpower the recalcitrant: the bailiffs were sent in. Why not? Public opinion was opposed to all vital religion and what savoured of mysticism, pietism and pharisaism. It was not offended in any way by this excessive use of power. In fact it often seemed almost to smile and cheer at the penalties and embarrassments of those weird and obstinate devotees. When I found that I could no longer remain a passive witness to this glaring injustice, though I disapproved of dissent and regarded precipitous separation as extremely injurious to the interests of the church, I finally broke my guilty silence. Fiercely repulsed at first, my pleas gradually struck a chord; persecution waned and the dissenters' situation was mollified. But it was not until 1852 that dissent was recognised and legalised.

Now then, was it in the name of the Canons of Dordt that I pleaded for them? No, initially I protested against the outlawing of any form of worship; next I stood up for substance as opposed to form, for lawful order as opposed to legal order, unity of doctrine as opposed to unity of regulation. I pointed out that the church was not an assembly of persons subject to the same external forms of public worship, but—in Mr Berryer's fine definition—"An association of souls bound together by the same beliefs about God."[58] The bond and rule of a church, I said, is the faith it professes. These people you are pursuing, even into their private meetings, should have been able to find in the church what, in desperation, they now hope to find by leaving it. After invading their homes, do not lay hold of them as if they were serfs of a territory you had invaded. After violating their rights, at least let their conscience go free. Here the confessional and legal perspective exposed the enormity of a persecution in which church and state, hand in glove, hounded the owner from his house, and then denied him refuge or shelter anywhere else.

If we wanted the right to disapprove of dissent, we had to demonstrate the same spirit of zeal and sacrifice without becoming separatists ourselves. If we wanted to remain within a church that had been invaded by unbelief, we could not remain idle—though out of a sense of duty, not self-interest—without rendering our motives highly problematic. We had to insist on the restoration of discipline and the maintenance of doctrine. Hence our address to the Synod in 1842.

---

[58] Pierre-Antoine Berryer (1790–1868), French Catholic lawyer and politician. The provenance of the quotation is unknown.

What was its meaning, purpose, and scope? In response to many who had petitioned them to restore the authority of the Confession of Faith, the Synod interpreted their perfectly just requests in the most absurd and ridiculous manner, and with a wry arrogance, disdainfully rejected them. At the same time, and as if there had been no cause for complaint and the opposition was quibbling over trifles, it decided to add that, under the new arrangements, the ancient foundations of the Reformed church had not been in the least disturbed, and that its leading and vital doctrines were clearly still a mandatory requirement for its pastors.

On the strength of this declaration, we felt the need for urgent intervention and for a rejoinder. We agree with you, we said, we could not ask for anything more; but how can you square what you *say* with the *actual* denial of the authority of Scripture, of the divinity of Christ, and of the forgiveness of sins by the blood of the cross? Must we conclude from your indifference that the truths that encapsulate the faith of our forefathers, and which are our only comfort in life and in death, have, in your judgement and that of modern science, little value? Who is to be the judge in the church of what is fundamental and what is secondary? Do you want to leave this to the good pleasure of each minister? In that case, your statement, while fine in appearance, will end in the dissolution of the church, by causing absolute subjectivism to reign there. So please explain your thinking; examine whether your statements might not be specious. Do you really desire to maintain what, in our confessional standards, are deemed, in the judgement of those who wrote them, essential, and in keeping with the historic faith of the Dutch Reformed Church?

At the same time we broached an issue of the utmost importance: theological education in the universities. Historically the Faculty of Theology was specifically intended to train ministers in the Reformed religion. Through every political change, this goal had remained the same. But by a singular anomaly, even after the supposed separation of church and state, the appointment of professors continued to be undertaken by the government and, in a much graver confusion of ideas, appointments were based solely on academic attainments, with no regard to personal beliefs. Thus, at the University of Groningen, the school reduced the Gospel to the dimensions of an updated Platonism, infiltrated every pulpit, and reigned unopposed. Again, we are not toying with the idea of inflicting a subtle and narrow Calvinism; but, standing on the same broad, firm ground we had already chosen, we said: Either close the Faculty of Theology and let the church erect and manage its own seminaries, or put the appointment of professors in the hands of the ecclesiastical authorities. If you refuse to choose between these two options; if, despite such an obvious confusion of powers, the state persists in reserving to itself a task as important as it is difficult and sensitive, then at least ensure that it acts in accordance with the interests and rights of the church, and not hand over its young Levites, in the name of a science falsely so called, to the cleverest and the most ardent enemies of its faith.

Finally, among the great concerns of the church, we had to pay attention to *primary education* in particular. The law of 1806 permanently settled a mixed school system on us; this increasingly came under the influence of the rationalists and Catholics. In most districts, any direct religious teaching was effectively banned and replaced with a *mongrel* religion that Mr de Gasparin referred to as "an attenuated and insipid religion, reduced to mere morality, lacking that salt the Gospel speaks of, of no use or value to anyone."[59] How could we, to some extent at least, offset the deplorable consequences of such a system? Only one way was open to us: alongside the flawed public schools we had to take refuge in private education. But this was no simple matter. Prior approval was mandatory, and this permission was almost always refused by the local authorities for fear of effective competition and antipathy to what they saw as the excesses of an unhealthy zeal.

---

[59] *Intérêts généraux du Protestantisme Français*, p. 557.

It is difficult to convey an idea of the tenacity and specious reasoning of those supporters of the mixed school (which they regarded as the guarantee of public peace and national unity) who opposed us for many years before 1857. In vain, by an order of 2nd January 1842, in which he ruefully confirmed the absence of religious teaching in public schools (already implied in the idea of a mixed school), King William II tried to offer some relief from a monopoly that was become increasingly repressive and unjust. The liberal Protestant party knew how to evade, and even put a false construction on, his well-intentioned provisions. In The Hague they went so far as to insist that no private school could be licensed unless it too was mixed and entirely conformed to the public school, turning authorisation into the bizarre privilege of paying for a school that was just like the one we were trying to escape. From 1844 to 1849, all our efforts against this monstrous sophism failed at every level of government. What should we do now? We argued our case from the confessional perspective. We laid emphasis on the fact that the church and its members had a right and a duty to give their children not only catechetical instruction, but an education in keeping with its doctrines and its precepts. Did this mean we wanted to bring into the classroom the doctrinal subtleties of our Reformed Church or a particularism that other churches formed during the Reformation would not tolerate? Quite the contrary. Our schools have consistently demonstrated that our aim has been to meet the needs of all Protestant denominations, and to oppose an insignificant and sentimental religiosity with a positive teaching of the grand facts of the Gospel and their influence on the minds and hearts of our children.

Having thus surveyed our conduct between 1837 and 1848, it will not be amiss to make clear—by general considerations and by referring back to what we have already said about our confessional viewpoint—the nature and grounds of our efforts.

To begin with, we faced danger and urgency. Suffice it to say that Mr Gaussen's severe strictures in 1831 with regard to the church of

I. The Orthodox Confessional Party

Geneva were, to say the least, just as applicable to our church: "The three most fatal errors that have successively ravaged the church in days gone by—Arianism in the fourth century, Pelagianism in the fifth and Socinianism in the sixteenth—have joined forces in Geneva; but now they are not acting alone, through a few individuals, and clandestinely—they have taken over public education. They are even fighting there over the doctrine of the expiation of the sins of the world through the blood of atonement."[60]

Second, a sudden change seemed neither possible nor desirable. We felt we needed to revive a sense of right and duty in believers to keep the church to the fundamentals of its faith. In 1847, I summed up our attitude in response to the following question: Do you want the ministers of the church who attack its fundamental beliefs to be summarily dismissed? No, I said, what we want to do is revive a sense of the church's right to not be attacked and betrayed by those whose mission it is to defend it. The problems of truth and error and of life and death in the church are not just a legal issue; they are mainly a problem of sickness and the recuperation it needs. If we are going to cleanse the body, we cannot begin by dismantling it. And I expressed our thinking clearly in a few lines in *L'Espérance*: "We do not believe this approach is ever appropriate in the Christian church, and especially at this time. It has all the appearance of being very simple and direct, but this simplicity is entirely mechanical and pragmatic. When to some extent or other, every part of a body has succumbed to a serious illness we should not rush immediately to the extremes of surgery and amputation to cure it. All of us who believe that we possess truth and life to some degree or other should nurture and develop it in our own lives and transmit it to those around us so that, as if being passed from fibre

---

[60]*Assemblée Générale de la Société Évangélique de Genève, tenue le 18 juin 1840 a l'Oratoire. Neuvième Anniversaire* (Geneva: Imprimerie de Jules-G.me Fick, 1840), p. 18.

to fibre and artery to artery, the most remote, lifeless, and numb parts will be gradually revived."[61]

Thirdly, far from wanting to enslave the conscience, we were the true defenders of freedom. Outside the church, we advocate the greatest possible degree of liberty for everyone in the sphere of individual rights; in the church, we advocate a rule of teaching as the only way to guarantee the believer's liberty against the pastor's licence, against his substituting his own doctrines and dreams for the faith of the flock.

Finally, we have never had recourse to the state. We have never invoked the secular arm. We have protested against partiality and the continual intervention of the temporal power, which has decided to discover the Reformed Church not in its faith but in the anti-Presbyterian regulations it has imposed on a Presbyterian church by royal decree.

The nature and scope of our defence of the church's rights in the States General

The year 1848 brought about great changes in the political constitution of the realm and in the electoral system. I myself entered the States General. Similarly, in 1850, direct elections brought in two of my friends, and later, in 1853, four of them.

Did my friends and I abuse our parliamentary position? Did we try to cajole the civil power, either to lend its support to the unreasonable demands of the confessional party in the internal government of the Reformed Church, or to grant this church any kind of primacy or advantage in its relations with the state?

Nothing of the sort. We asked for the emancipation and freedom of the church. And against what have we constantly protested? Against an arbitrary regime that, with illusory promises of a future separation, continues to impose its very real yoke; against an organisation of the church that is contrary to its principles and traditions;

---

[61]No. 85, 24 October 1843.

I. The Orthodox Confessional Party

against its subjugation under oligarchic forms; against its identification with this governmental straitjacket; against the government's conduct in making common cause with the enemies of the church, who are protected by regulatory provisions and are past masters of insolent attack and underhand scheming. We demanded impartiality and neutrality; we never sought the favour of the temporal power for the orthodox party.

In addition, we have unreservedly resigned ourselves to the situation in which we have been placed, since 1795, by the overthrow of the privileged church. Committed, without reserve or regret, to equality of worship, we have never tried to regain those special privileges, even when the opportunity appeared favourable. The events of 1853 demonstrated our selflessness and sincerity. The sudden publication of a papal bull for the introduction of bishops caused a violent commotion in the country and, by its offensive disdain in particular, gave the Protestant spirit a boost. Certainly, we showed our surprise at the singular contrast between a *laissez-faire* approach (one of no restrictions whatsoever) towards the Catholic Church, and the indefinite prolongation of government intervention into the spiritual concerns of the Reformed Church. We argued the case for safeguards against the encroachments of ultramontanism, which at that very moment was resuming its haughty and menacing attitude in several European countries. But at the same time, we resisted attempts to induce the States General to adopt legislative measures—clearly intended to target Catholics—to set up a surveillance and control force [haute police] that would have been detrimental to the principles of true freedom. While scrupulously respecting the rights of the Roman Church, we obtained modifications to the bill, in the interests of all the churches, which brought that church within the bounds of the legitimate powers of the civil authorities.

As soon as I entered the House, in 1849, I summarised my principles on the independence and influence of churches in relation to the state. There was here, I said, a two-fold perspective. First, the church is an independent corporation. Like all other corporations, it is subject to the state's supervision, with equal right to its general protection. But it is autonomous, and spurns all interference within the sphere of its private concerns. Nevertheless, churches are inextricably tied in to public affairs; they have their own characteristic influence on the state, which the state cannot disregard without putting itself at odds with the nation. In systems of state religion, the sovereign or the political unit imposes its beliefs on public institutions as a rule. Now, a genuine separation of church and state imposes on the sovereign an obligation, in everything relating to religious concerns and needs, to harmonise the public institutions with the nation's beliefs, not his own or the state's. Its concern now is not the religion of the government, but the religion of the governed.

That was the theory; a very simple one I believe, but the one by which I felt we had to be guided. Leaving aside the disputed question of a Christian state, I said: In any case, remember that you are the government of a *Christian* people. So, wherever the issue is about religion, directly or indirectly, take account of the nation's beliefs. Suppress—provided that you have the right—suppress out of duty such abuses as Christianity condemns. Promote the emancipation of slaves; in your colonies, do not hamper missionary work by giving Mohammedanism and paganism your endorsement, or by raising them to the rank of privileged religions. Above all, do not be tempted to believe that you have a right to organise your institutions in opposition to popular beliefs. Neither should you take the next step and suppose it either lawful or necessary to forget that Christianity is the hallmark of this nation. At this stage, I do not intend to examine the responsibility or consequences of such forgetfulness. There can be no question that at all times you are to govern in the interests of a *religious* people. In whatever situation that religion is a necessary element, you may neither banish it nor replace it with a syncretism of your own making. You may not impose on the people either *atheist* institutions or a *mixed civil* religion.

I. The Orthodox Confessional Party

If you treat this vital distinction with contempt, you will give the green light to political absolutism and state omnipotence. From the moment you start down this path, your organic laws, your reforms, and your new institutions will culminate in the creation of a government machine that will destroy everything which the nation—the historical family, or what you call the sovereign people—holds most dear and most sacred.

The practical importance of this idea has been felt in the laws on primary education and public welfare.

In education, we started from this principle and took our stand on an axiom derived from it. For the vast majority, even the freedom to set up *private* schools is not enough; what they also insist on, and insist on above everything else, is a *public* school system that reflects the religious needs of the nation.

Similarly, on the issue of poverty, we felt that the state should not only respect the independence of the churches, but that it should also acknowledge their support; that Christian charity should not be regulated, nor its streams of benevolence dried up by public assistance; that systematic taxation for the sake of the poor should be rigorously eschewed, and pauperism should not be made the object of the public purse by recognising, at least indirectly, a right to the state's assistance.

Education and charity: these domains belong to the church, or at the very least the state should not lay claim to them as its own. It cannot set itself up as sole teacher and grand almoner of the nation without stripping the church of its rights and duties. What we have here are simple corollaries of the spiritual power's nature and mission, and every church in which a living heart beats has always resisted the usurpations of the secular arm on these great issues.

Confusion of church and state?

This summary will, I hope, be sufficient to show that in our defence of the rights and liberties of the Reformed Church we have neither made exaggerated claims nor dragged religion into the arena of sordid interests and petty passions. However, on more general considerations, a very serious attack has been mounted against us. The confessional party, it is said, has become a political party. Under the name of the *Anti-Revolutionary Party* it has embroiled itself in legislative issues. By trying to engage on two fronts, it has imperceptibly confused two orders of ideas that ought to have been kept strictly separate. This two-fold engagement has had dire consequences.

It is no longer Mr Trottet we have to deal with here. We have to respond to other detractors—to compatriots who have long shared our views and taken part in our struggles, but who, in recent years, have taken a different path. They have largely blamed our exaggeration, our rigid traditional viewpoint, and our reactionary ultraconservative mentality, for the disunion among friends of the Gospel and the failure of their own labours.

I can best summarise their assessment of us by citing the words of Mr Chantepie de la Saussaye[62] as an example, for by his faith, piety, knowledge and philosophical spirit, he occupies a prominent place among the theologians of our country. After I had been appointed head of the Anti-Revolutionary Party in 1858, he made the following solemn pronouncement to a meeting of evangelical pastors in December 1859:

> You know, brethren, I could not join the Anti-Revolutionary Party, as a political party, without reservations. However, never was I able to see, as I see today, how contrary the tendency of its principles is to the highest order of history, where a more powerful arm than man's, by ways that man would not have chosen—that is, by revolutions, changes and upheavals—has preserved, maintained and unfolded all that is good and true, eternal and divine, and thereby brought forth a richer strain of life. Never have I so powerfully felt,

---

[62]Daniël Chantepie de la Saussaye (1818–1874), Dutch Reformed clergyman and theologian, founder of the so-called Ethical school.

either, the danger—for the salvation of man's soul and the maintenance and prosperity of the church—from forcing the everlasting Gospel into fleeting forms and from identifying a political and ecclesiastical conservatism with the interests of the kingdom of God, which has always spread and advanced through the storms of universal history.

These are not expressions blurted out by our friend in the heat of an argument or in an impromptu speech. He uttered this harsh sentence after mature consideration, in a written account that was constructed with great care, and in which he set out his reasons for leaving the world of the periodical press after six years in it.

We are accused of mixing religion and politics. We believe that we have acted on one and the same principle with regard to both church and state. We are accused of having preached an extreme conservatism. We believe that we have simply been faithful to the Gospel. I will try to develop these ideas in a separate chapter.

II. THE ANTI-REVOLUTIONARY PRINCIPLE

What is the Revolution?

Coming as it does from *Christian* friends, this charge gives us good grounds for astonishment. The Anti-Revolutionary Party, they say, injures both religion and politics, because it insists on confusing what should be kept distinct and separate. Now, why—after having wholeheartedly embraced evangelical beliefs—why do they not see that the prevailing spirit of our times has its origin and raison d'être in a rejection of *revealed* truth?

Why do they not see that the overthrow of the religious, political, and social order was not the result of a revolutionary *blip*, but of a revolutionary *condition,* and that *perpetual revolution* always has been and always will be the inevitable consequence of the denial of man's dependence on the God of nature, history and the Gospel?

Why do they not see that this evil cannot be brought to an end by attacking merely its symptoms? It has to be torn up by the roots.

Why do they not see that the only antidote for systematic unbelief is faith?

Why do they not see that the anti-revolutionary principle is nothing other than the Protestant Christian principle, the *Reformation* principle? It alone—*standing on revelation and history*—can successfully combat this anti-religious, anti-social principle. It alone, *through the Gospel*, can realise whatever there is of truth and goodness in these revolutionary utopias, and so save both church and state.

The easiest way of bringing out the nature and meaning of the anti-revolutionary principle is to answer the question: *What is the Revolution?* For, if we can come to an understanding of *that*, then we can draw from its features the distinctive traits of the principle needed to combat it.

Someone recently said, and with a good deal of truth: "The historical sciences seem destined to replace the abstract philosophy of the schools as a solution to the problems that now most passionately engage the human mind.... The history of the human mind is the true philosophy of our time. Nowadays any question quickly sinks into a historical debate; every exposition of principles becomes a history lesson. Each of us is what he is only in terms of his historically-formed system." So said Ernest Renan;[63] and I have no hesitation in applying even the last sentence to my situation, because for him the Christian faith is just one more system among countless others, so that I too am what I am only as a product of my historically-formed system, that is, by my acceptance of the testimony of the Scriptures to the living God. In this Christian sense, I have constantly appealed to history in my evaluation of the Revolution. Not, indeed, with a view to moulding it, in line with preconceived notions, into an arbitrary framework; but in order to try and understand and describe, in light of the actual facts, the nature and outworking of its dominant ideas, which are just so many facts of an intangible and higher order, under the dominance of which the course of events and the fate of peoples are determined and set in motion. In its essence, the Revolution is a single great historical fact: the invasion of the human mind by the doctrine of the absolute sovereignty of man, thus making him the source and centre of all truth, by substituting human reason and human will for divine revelation and divine law. The Revolution is the history of the irreligious philosophy of the past century; it is, in its origin and outworking, the doctrine that—given free rein—destroys church and state, society and family, produces disorder without ever establishing liberty or restoring moral order, and, in religion, inevitably leads its conscientious followers into atheism and despair. The anti-revolutionary principle is

---

[63] *Essais de morale et de critique* [Essays on Morality and Criticism] (Paris: M. Lévy Frères, 1860), pp. 82, 83.

II. The Anti-Revolutionary Principle 41

the polar opposite of the Revolution; it is the Gospel and history that, in the name of religion, law, progress, and liberty, resist anarchy.

Now if there still exist, especially among many of our friends, misunderstandings in this regard, if I am suspected of hankering after a petty reactionary conservatism, it is not for lack of having frequently and plainly explained myself.

It is now thirty years since I first drew attention to the dangers of revolutionary currents. Entirely unique circumstances, at the beginning of my political career, allowed me to see, through the dizzying atmosphere of a deceptive liberalism, the key to the anarchy of mind and continuous upheaval of our time. The year was 1829. A revolutionary crisis in France and the Netherlands was imminent. As Cabinet Secretary to King William I, I could see the storm brewing in both Brussels and The Hague; I was present at the increasingly violent deliberations of the States General; I avidly read and scoured the newspapers and leaflets, and closely followed the passionate battle in the press. I took a lively interest in the growing threats to my country and, while fully aware of the danger, I wanted to take part in the conflict. I was concerned about the course of events, concerned above all by the government's silence and indecision as well as the apathy of the Dutch public, which was so slow in responding. And so, while not leaving the King in the dark, and fully prepared to sacrifice the advantages of my social position, I published a kind of political magazine, or rather opposition magazine, in which I endeavoured to draw the serious attention of my compatriots to the nature of the difficulties of which we were both witnesses and victims. I was being imperceptibly led to reflect on the root causes of the general disturbance. The situation in Europe seemed to me to be the consequence of false doctrines, the consequence and price of contempt for the fundamental laws of humanity, and of the systematic undermining of social relations. It was the fruit of the Revolution, in the strictest and most significant sense of the word.

Its history

In 1831, my beliefs with regard to this unique character of our time were settled. I then tried to summarise them in a sketch of history since 1789, presented as the practical development of an unbelieving philosophy, as revolutionary theory in action.

The following, more or less, is how, by surveying the recent woefully fertile fifty years of agitation and misfortune, I tried to follow the thread through this labyrinth.

The Revolution's principle is the idolatrous worship of humanity; man recognises no one but himself as sovereign, nothing but his reason as light, nothing but his will as the rule; he worships man and dethrones God. It advocates the abolition of all social ties and the establishment of universal licence; an unprecedented state of affairs, which necessarily leads, through related notions, to the last stages of doubt in religion and the dissolution of society in politics.

But there are aspects of man's nature that cannot be expunged, even by his errors and fads. He needs a God, so he takes refuge in deism; he needs to live among his fellows, so he creates an artificial society by striving to create the ultimate utopia of modern public law, Rousseau's *Social Contract*.[64]

From the revolutionary point of view, this is the only legitimate society. From the concurrence of individual wills is born the general will, by the vote of the numerical majority. Every government, as representative of the people, is responsible for the execution of its mandate. Unlimited equality and freedom, democracy and universal brotherhood, these are now, under whatever guise, the pattern and ideal in politics.

No doubt an admirable plan, if only man could abandon his passions and vices. Rousseau, despite the reservations his own history and

---

[64]Jean-Jacques Rousseau (1712–1778), Swiss political philosopher.

II. The Anti-Revolutionary Principle

confessions suggested to him, persisted in taking his starting point in the innate goodness of man. He wrote, with more truth than he apparently believed: "If there were a people made up of Gods, it would govern itself democratically; so perfect a government is not suitable for men."[65] Elsewhere he says: "This is the great problem to be solved in politics: to find a form of government that puts the law above man. If such a form cannot be found — and I frankly confess I think it can't — I think we should go to the opposite extreme and put one man as far above the law as we can, and consequently create the most arbitrary despotism possible. I would like the despot to be a God. In short, I see no middle way between the most severe democracy and the most perfect Hobbism. For the conflict between men and laws, which puts the state into perpetual civil war, is the worst of all political states."[66]

There is no better proof of the natural course of that fatal and ungodly teaching, of which this eloquent sophist was the most fervent apostle, despite his attempts at disavowal. Yes, certainly, we need to find a law above man; and so it must be a law that man did not make. But this law — revealed law, divine law — you have abolished, and in addition to creating disorder, anarchy, a *bellum omnium contra omnes* [a war of all against all], you have to admit that, as a result of your sublime efforts, you have no security against social convulsion other than arbitrariness and force.

This admission of his was prophetic; it is the very epitome of the history of the Revolution. It is a beam that sheds light on the cause of its mistakes and disasters, and the latter are but the natural fruit of the triumphant Revolution. But its apparent triumph is no more than a perpetual denial of its false promises.

---

[65] *Social Contract*, Book III, chapter iv.

[66] Jean-Jacques Rousseau, *Lettres philosophiques,* ed. Henri Gaston Gouhier (Paris: J. Vrin, 1974), Letter 47, p. 168. Also in *Correspondance: Nouvelle édition augmentée,* Arvensa éditions, p. 1444 (Letter DCCLXXXI – to Mirabeau, 26 July 1767).

Its development has been logical and the only opposition it has encountered has been from within its own bosom.

So what actually happened? How did the struggle come about? Did everyone agree that the Revolutionary principle had to be combatted? Quite the contrary. Time and again we lauded its doctrine to the skies; we believed we were witnessing in it the birth of a glorious new day. It was only when all public and private rights were seen to be threatened in France and throughout Europe that conflict broke out between the different interests and beliefs, between unswerving loyalty and wavering moderation. And once matters reached the stage of trying to implement these speculative notions, discord was not long in raising its head. For the delusional infatuations did not break down the barriers that nature—which is much stronger than man—put in the way of those who misunderstood her. The edge of the abyss was quickly reached, and if those among the revolutionaries who were not spellbound or carried away by blind zeal did not step back from the precipice, at least they halted and refused to move. And the more animated the movement became, the more energetic did desperate resistance become. In such cases, especially in such cases, extreme liberty leads to extreme tyranny. While we are agreed on the theory, we argued about how to implement it, to what extent and when. Hence the continual oscillation between a freedom that, recognising no boundaries, is mere licence, and an order that, having no moral fulcrum, is mere despotism. At each turn war breaks out, but it is always a civil war among the revolutionaries, in the very bosom of the Revolution itself.

The revolutions of 1789, 1793, and 1830 were only different phases of a single phenomenon, different acts of the same drama, "governmental revolutions within the Revolution."[67]

---

[67] Joseph Fiévée, *Correspondance et relations de J. Fiévée avec Bonaparte pendant onze années 1802 à 1813* [Correspondence and relations of J. Fiévée with Bonaparte for 11 years from 1802 to 1813] (Paris, Desrez, 1836), Volume 1, p. 106. The exact sentence

II. The Anti-Revolutionary Principle

Though we shuddered at the memory of the Terror and Jacobin propaganda, and later at the violence and conquests of the Empire, we believed—on the basis of the so-called wise concessions of a moderate liberalism—that we could prevent the return of these terrible calamities. We took for excess what were in fact direct consequences. We saw only fervent exaggeration, or a guilty denial of a salutary principle, in all these horrors and calamities; but they were the direct consequences of a fatal principle that was sometimes encouraged, sometimes arrested, in its natural outworking. Every concession was only a down-payment for more of the same; every attempt at moderation and balance, far from ending violent revolution, only prepared for its return and accelerated its progress.

At times, weary of alternative systems, we flattered ourselves that we could end the Revolution by a resistance that boldly sacrificed the interests of freedom to the exigencies of order. What happened? We only stayed its course by doubling its strength; the very act of placing a dyke across the path of a river only serves to make the river irresistible, for eventually the dyke must succumb to the ever-increasing fierceness of turbulent water. We feed the evil we want to throttle. "A spirit of reaction foments a spirit of revolution."[68]

What is the real remedy for such a state of affairs? We must strike the evil at its root. We must completely abandon this independent subjectivism; it has no concern for God's sovereignty or for man's fall and

---

is: "The more the French saw governmental revolutions following one another in what one calls the Revolution, the more a guarantee of stability produced by those revolutions, was impressed upon them." Fiévée (1767–1839) was a French journalist and writer, and counsellor to Napoleon.

[68] Guizot, *Pourquoi la révolution d'Angleterre a-t-elle réussi? Discours sur l'histoire de la révolution d'Angleterre* [Why did the English revolution succeed? discourse on the history of the English revolution] (Brussels: Meline, Cans & Co., 1850), p. 70. The complete quotation is "The spirit of reaction, that malady of winning parties, incessantly foments the spirit of revolution."

weakness, it undermines the foundation of all truth, and it is forever tearing down without ever being able to rebuild. We must embrace once again immutable truths now long-forgotten. We must submit to divine authority. We must return to the Christian principle.

Do not be deceived by appearances. This is not about material interests or national interests, forms of government or differences between confessions of faith, let alone about the struggle between the spirit of conservation and the spirit of progress. It is about resisting or obeying the God of the Gospel, the Living God. Abjure human pride. It desires only its own sovereignty, and remakes religion and society in its own image; it is bent on destroying all that itself has not created or sanctioned. Repudiate lawless sophistry, and you will find yourself back on the terra firma of history and reality.

But what shall we say? Was the French, or rather European, Revolution not justified? Were we bound to perpetuate crumbling institutions? Were we bound to cling superstitiously to the forms and relics of a feudal system? Were we bound to resign ourselves to every whim of arbitrary power, and to submit with a passive indifference to every phase of decay? Certainly not. The situation in France and across Europe called loudly for a reformation. But it did not make desirable or even inevitable the very opposite of a reformation: an anti-religious revolution, a revolution in the fundamental ideas of social order; one that overthrows—under the guise of reforming abuse—even the most useful institutions, and one that denies—under the guise of combatting prejudice—even the most sacred principles.

Must we then renounce the hopes we had in 1789? Must we consign freedom, equality, brotherhood, tolerance, humanity, and progress to a systematic condemnation? Is there no truth to these ideas? It would be absurd to suppose so. They echo, in part, the noblest aspirations and legitimate desires of the human heart. But, if our happiness is to be assured, it is not enough profusely to scatter fine maxims that have been divorced from the supreme truth that alone can make them effective. The Revolution that proclaimed them infused them with sterility, or to be more exact, it denatured them. These ideas, branches detached from the Gospel tree and poisoned by revolutionary sap, bear but deadly fruit. In the service of an anti-Christian philosophy, even a panacea only compounds the evil, it does not heal.

Corruptio optimi pessima [the corruption of the best is the worst of corruptions]. The great ideas of 1789 were eagerly embraced and at the time had all the appearances, when contrasted with the current meanness and immorality, of impartiality and superiority. In and of themselves these ideas were irreproachable and in complete conformity with the source of all genuine truth, but because of their ties to the unbelief that ruled the mind of the times, they were nevertheless bound to turn out fatal. Just because of their relative goodness, they were bound to spark into life a fanaticism that felt justified in sacrificing everything on the altar of its own sublime conceptions. And after it had given birth, in the pursuit of its chimerical schemes, and by the most atrocious means, to the crimes of the Terror, this bloody perversity was itself broken by an iron sceptre. The despotic rule of Bonaparte was the inevitable outcome of the dictatorship of Robespierre.

I applied myself to identifying the revolutionary principle in all its governmental forms from 1789 to 1831, and to demonstrating the instability of any power that thinks it has found the key to combat them in a supposedly moderate application of anarchic maxims. From 1789 to 1795 the Revolution pursued its course; from 1795 to 1814 it turned on itself. This reaction found its highest expression in the Empire, as the original movement did its own in the Terror. The Restoration was little more than a change of personnel in favour of an emancipated liberalism, bringing back the old dynasty to continue the work begun in 1789. The Bourbon government was called upon to reign, for good or ill, with the revolutionary institutions and along liberal lines, in keeping with Napoleon's dictum: "I am the bookmark that marks the page where the Revolution was halted; but when I am gone, it will turn over the page and resume its march." The constitution, now interpreted in a liberal sense, was still at bottom—as it had been under the Empire—republicanism, centralised democracy, and popular sovereignty; but now under the parliamentary forms that Napoleon had extinguished and that we, in good faith, wanted to revive. Liberalism had only to draw out the consequences of the constitution thus interpreted in order to cast aside or overturn the throne. As I said as early as 1831, we would watch it act out its comedy for fifteen years or so before it reached its tragic denouement. The monarchy of 1830 resumed, but under much more difficult conditions, the task of resistance that had been so abruptly interrupted. An elected king, a citizen king, a monarchy surrounded by republican institutions and with doubtful claims, as well as a legal opposition, had together shaken the established order and changed its character; they now combined to call into question the new government's legitimacy. Casimir Périer[69] located the secret of its strength in a wholesome fear of radicalism; but as fear subsided, opposition to it came to life again. And the more order appeared to be settled, the more the vehemence of the extreme party—which was impervious to reason—made the crisis and subsequent collapse inevitable, as it had done before.

Finally I pointed to a powerless Europe. Dominated by the evil that had surfaced in France, it embraced the principle (though it shrank from the appalling results of its practice) of applauding all systems that appeared to reconcile faith and self-interest and, as payment for its complicity with revolutionary France, was doomed to submit by turns to the conqueror's armed propaganda and the point of his sword. The Revolution was not a peculiarly French phenomenon, as Renan supposed, but rather a universal phenomenon of the modern world. France may have given birth to it, but despite the shared principles and currents across Europe, it was a phenomenon fatally hostile to the other powers, and for the simplest of reasons: it was there that it broke

---

[69]First minister to King Louis Philippe (who reigned from 1830 to 1848).

out and immediately displayed its aggressive and destructive character, thus forcing Europe to arm itself against such an horrendous menace.

Such seemed, to me, to be the results of the first practical demonstration of last century's philosophy.

Anarchistic contradictions

I dealt with the same subject at greater length back in 1847, in a book whose title epitomised my viewpoint: *Unbelief and Revolution*. Unbelief is the seed; revolution is the fruit.

In the last analysis, what do the magnificent promises made by the Revolution for the happiness of mankind amount to? They amount to a tyranny of the majority by whatever means; they amount to tyrannical power. And what will these fine promises of liberty eventually come to? To an unrestricted yet legal slavery; to what is utterly destructive of all liberty: the absolutism or omnipotence of the state; to a centralised power that sweeps away every private and public form of life, and covers and conceals all its injustice and tyranny with the veil of the common weal. Administrative centralisation existed in France under the *ancien régime;* but the Revolution, which assumed its forms, gave it an entirely different character. It is no longer a political mechanism, but a social principle. Every government, be it personal or parliamentary, becomes the form in which the state—as the lawful country, as the sovereign people, and as the general will or organised assembly of individual wills—is concentrated. The adage: *I am the State! (l'État c'est moi!)* acquires a much more frightening aspect than ever it had before. The government *is* the state, and the state is the social contract realised. Its decrees, properly understood, "boils down to simply this: the total absorption of each and every person with all his rights in the community as a whole. The general will is always right. Whoever refuses obedience to the general will shall be compelled to do so by the whole body, which means he will be forced to be free."[70] Liberty consists in doing what we do not necessarily will, because it is what we are legally bound to will. There are no rights against this right. The state is sovereign and the will of him who represents the state—which is sovereign in every sphere of life, even in the family and the conscience—breaks all resistance in the unity of its demands. "The sovereignty of the people has two aspects. Considered in its formation, it elevates every individual, making them members of the sovereign people. Considered in its application, it crushes and destroys them. No one has rights over against the right that proceeds from all."[71] The regime of liberty becomes, in its revolutionary simplicity, the legal organisation of the most complete tyranny.

To such a public legal order, we have to oppose *divine legitimacy* and *divine right*.

We mean *legitimacy* in its broadest and most incontrovertible sense. "There are things that are sacred, inviolable, and legitimate. They come under the aegis of universal justice; they can never change, and cannot be set aside by any human power. This is the principle of legitimacy in its highest universality. [By contrast, where] there is no universal justice; [where] there is nothing sacred, nothing inviolable, nothing legitimate; [where] all laws can be changed to suit the will of the sovereign and the sovereign is he who is most powerful; [then] all rights can be sacrificed to the public interest and the public interest is whatever we say it is. Such is the principle of illegitimacy or revolution in all its august majesty."[72]

---

[70]Three separate quotations from Rousseau combined, from *Du contrat social* [Social Contract]: first sentence, Bk I, ch. 6; second sentence, Bk II, ch. 2; third sentence, Bk I, ch. 7.

[71]A. E. de Gasparin, *Intérêts généraux du Protestantisme Français* [General Interests of Protestantism in France] (Paris, Librairie de L-R. Delay, 1843), p. 581.

[72]*Journal des Débats*, 1818.

II. The Anti-Revolutionary Principle

Divine right: but not in the sense of a Jewish theocracy, nor in the absurd sense of the Stuarts, nor in the sense of Hobbes'[73] servility, nor yet as interpreted by Bonaparte. Rather, we mean divine right as it was understood before the advent of the Revolution: as the basis of all government, republican or monarchical, and as the only adequate foundation for every right and every liberty. "All genuine law comes from God, who is the eternal principle of communal order and power in any society of intelligent beings. Apart from such, all we have are capricious wills and a humiliating reign of violence; men insolently lording it over other men; nothing but slaves and tyrants. And so all social verities are derived from this grand primary verity: *all power comes from God.*"[74]

The choice is inescapable. Deny this fundamental truth, and you are forced to explain by purely human conventions the source, not so much of powers (history furnishes more than enough examples of this), but of *the very notion of power*. We have to choose between the sovereignty of man and the sovereignty of God. Reject sovereignty by the grace of God and you are left with nothing but radicalism. Without divine right, there is no genuine authority, whether kingly, parliamentary or republican; these names offer nothing but a state of revolution, where force upholds one party and puts down another, while being itself at every turn the central power. There is no other option: you can have anarchy and servitude as the products of a *social contract*, or you can find the source of rights and liberty in the absolute and beneficial authority of God.

---

[73]Thomas Hobbes (1588–1679), English political philosopher.

[74]F. R. de Lamennais, *Œuvres complètes de F. de La Mennais, tome 1: Essai sur l'indifférence en matière de religion* [Complete works of F. de Lamennais, vol. 1, Essay on indifference in matters of religion] (Paris, Paul Daubrée et Cailleux, 1836–1837), p. 309.

Witnesses old and new

Often and vigorously have I been reproached for attacking generally-received notions with too little tact; my opposition was seen as being excessively arrogant and eccentric. But, I said, we are dealing with fundamental verities here, belief in which admits neither hesitation nor doubt. Moreover, I brought forward from across the centuries a cloud of witnesses that would condemn the revolutionary principle.

Among the ancients, subjectivism found advocates only among the disreputable sophists. The Gospel and the Reformation drove it out; and though the weakening of faith in the eighteenth century did lead to its triumph, even then it only penetrated the minds of an elite among faith's opponents. When I cited contemporary authorities, I leaned towards the historical school of Savigny[75] and Niebuhr.[76] I pointed out what was admirable and informative, despite their ultramontanist errors, in the writings of Bonald,[77] de Maistre,[78] and not least, perhaps, in those of Lamennais[79] (though these already pointed forward to his complete apostasy). Above all, I tried to do justice to a most remarkable book, one that is rarely read among us, and even then only to be decried. I refer to Von Haller's *Restauration der Staats-Wissenschaft*

---

[75] Friedrich Karl von Savigny (1779–1861), German professor of law, founder of the Historical School of Jurisprudence.

[76] Barthold Georg Niebuhr (1776–1831), German historian, pioneer of the scientific method in historiography.

[77] Louis Gabriel Ambroise de Bonald (1754–1840), French counterrevolutionary writer and politician.

[78] Joseph de Maistre (1753–182), Savoyard counterrevolutionary writer and diplomat.

[79] Hugues Félicité Robert de Lamennais (1782–1854), French Catholic priest and writer, initially a proponent of counterrevolutionary philosophy, later converted to republicanism while also renouncing Christianity.

II. The Anti-Revolutionary Principle

[Restoration of Political Science].[80] On the negative side, I was struck by his refutation of liberalism. In his essentially historical presentation, he demonstrated how the right of hereditary personal monarchy has been infiltrated and distorted by theories of republican society; then, how the revolutionary principle embraced this error, in order to turn it into the social doctrine of popular sovereignty and universal democracy; and finally, how every right and every liberty was submerged, in the name of liberty, in the absolutism and omnipotence of the sovereign state. And in full accord with Ancillon, a writer who usually speaks with the utmost reserve, I found Von Haller admirable when he "strikes down and demolishes the false and dangerous doctrines of social contract and popular sovereignty."[81]

I was suspected of similar sympathies, but could happily quote, and quote with relish, the great English statesmen, the most determined opponents of revolutionary ideas. I was delighted to observe the perseverance of William Pitt and his school in their fight against the Jacobin system in all its various forms. I tried to point out the contrast between their loyalty to the basic principles of conservatism, and the conduct of the New Whigs, who were unfaithful to the noble traditions of 1688 and eagerly disseminated notions subversive of all social order. England watched as, in the name of freedom, they gave their support to imperial despotism and declaimed against war when war was clearly a national necessity. In attack they were reckless, in defence indiscriminate, in their prognostications false; they were wholly spellbound and driven by their party mantras.

In the meanwhile, their opponents stood firm, despite disappointment and disaster, and secured the triumph of Pitt's politics—as earlier they had William III's against Louis XIV—long after his death. I never

---

[80] Karl Ludwig von Haller (1768–1854). Swiss political philosopher.
[81] J.P.F. Ancillon, *Essais de philosophie, de politique et de littérature* (Paris: Gide, 1832), vol. III, p. 41. Ancillon (1767–1857) was a Prussian clergyman, historian, and convinced royalist.

tired of quoting Burke, "the Bossuet of politics," whom Fox (the most illustrious of his opponents) called a prophet without equal. A guide to Pitt himself, it was he who—when the French Revolution, at the beginning, produced an enchanting impression on almost all friends of liberty—first grasped the significance of the dreadful phenomenon; it was he who, by his example and influence, drew attention to the fundamental difference between 1688 and 1789, and created a sort of conservative Whiggism or constitutional Toryism, which became the focus of resistance in England; it was he who arrested the progress of the revolutionary spirit and nipped the spirit of conquest in the bud. "What we are witnessing," Burke said,[82] "and what we shall yet witness, is something extraordinary. This Revolution is unique. It is a revolution in ideas. It is the advent of a sect, a new religion. And this religion is just irreligion itself—godlessness, atheism, and hatred of Christianity erected into a system. It has started in chaos and will culminate in the most violent despotism; kings will be tyrants from policy when subjects are rebels from principle. War is inevitable. I am not attacking or thoughtlessly meddling in the French forms of government; I am mounting a defence against bellicose doctrines, against the dissemination of notions destructive of all government and society. It is civil war, and my aim is to give assistance to the true France and to save her from the clutches of a circle that would tyrannise her, that would use her as a jumping-off point and a support, that would make her the starting point and theatre of its designs and experiments, that aims at universal tyranny. Indeed, its very existence is a declaration of war against humanity. We are in a war between Christian civilisation and a wicked cosmopolitan ideology. Certain destruction awaits those

---

[82]This does not appear to be a direct quotation from Burke but a paraphrased summary of his thinking. One sentence seems to derive from the *Reflections of the Revolution in France*: "Kings will be tyrants from policy when subjects are rebels from principle."

II. The Anti-Revolutionary Principle

foolish princes who imagine they can negotiate war or peace by conventional means with this unique force. In this instance the path to salvation is the direct opposite of the beaten track. The most terrible war is a blessing in comparison; it would be a preservative against the spread and contagion of these false notions, and it would give the Christian world a breathing space."

I came to see that these statements and many others like them in his writings — often presented, it is true, in an enigmatic and paradoxical form — are anything but hyperbole. Rather, they cast a real light on the mystery of our century's strange crises, and a series of unprecedented calamities has demonstrated their complete accuracy. "The end of the Revolution indeed!" he exclaimed in 1798, when many thought it would end with the approaching peace with France, "The Revolution to finish indeed! It has hardly begun. So far, all you have heard is the overture, you have still to watch the full drama. Neither you nor I will see the final act of this drama." Burke drew his estimate of the tree from its roots, and so was able, with the sagacity of an incomparable statesman, to predict the progression of coming events. And if he made a mistake in 1789, when he thought the civil discord of the Revolution had destroyed France and wiped it off the map ("I see," he had said, "an abyss where France once stood"), he soon came to understand Mirabeau's reaction to it, and saw — perhaps better than Mirabeau himself did — that "this abyss is actually a volcano."

The lessons of modern history

In 1848, the revolutionary theory came to life again in the most radical expression of its practical outworking. A quasi-legitimate royalty — derived from popular sovereignty in action in 1830 but always shaky — died a sudden death as a result of the vice that had hardly been concealed since its institution. Its fall was the signal for a re-run of the first revolution on a reduced scale, but through all its phases and at an accelerated pace. It would be futile to catalogue them. We still remember that revolution, masquerading as a republic as it strove to establish itself again. It rushed headlong into all the logical absurdities of communism and socialism, and set about to engulf family and property within its factories and communes. But this dreadful uprising was driven back by the sound sense of society, which recoiled in horror at the approach of chaos. Order was re-established by force. The democratic state was smothered and replaced by martial law. The 24th February culminated three years later in the 2nd December, universal suffrage was strangled in a grip of steel, and the ephemeral Republic melted away before the reborn Empire. Another 18th Brumaire, another Napoleon, and the motto *in nepote redivivus* [in the nephew reborn] became a reality at home and abroad.

In France, the liberties of 1789 were unceremoniously consigned to an uncertain future, and the most extreme centralisation put at the immediate disposal of a single will. The throne was dressed in parliamentary garb, and the press forbidden to print anything that displeased the government. As peace had been the order of the day with the Consulate,[83] so also the Second Empire was essentially peaceful: "The Empire stands for peace." Peace was proclaimed, sincerely desired perhaps, but it was soon shattered, in the Crimea and in Italy, by such wars as the Christian world will hopefully never see again. The sickness in France, with its disasters, were once again contagious. Europe was embroiled in one great convulsion. For the most part, governments sought their preservation in measures that were at times violent, at others half-hearted, and cheerfully outstripped, in their deference and obsequiousness to French imperialism, what would have been regarded in the days of Napoleon I as the meanest form of royal and

---

[83]The Consulate was the government of France from the fall of the Directory in the coup of Brumaire, 1799, until the start of the Napoleonic Empire in 1804. Napoleon Bonaparte, as First Consul, was supported by Consuls Jean Jacques Régis de Cambacérès and Charles-François Lebrun.

diplomatic grovelling. Timidly they cocked an ear to catch what Paris said, only to take refuge in silence or parrot an answer.

Finally, we had *the rise of materialism*. The last embers of enthusiasm were dying in an atmosphere of equal indifference to truth and error, and of equal disdain for anything in the realm of ideas that jeopardised private interests or disrupted public order. Society gave itself over to the passionate and exclusive love of ease and security, happily sacrificing justice on the altar of personal well-being. It was indifferent to all else, recognising no distinctions but those of wealth and power, and no worship but that of lucre. This new order of things epitomised the spirit of the age, abolished any notion of good or evil, embraced crime as readily as virtue, and wreaked vengeance on any form of success. In its admirable simplicity, and in keeping with the most precise definition of this new legitimacy, it was nothing but the most barbaric expression of the law of the jungle substituted for the rule of public law and the law of nations.

We should not lose sight of the fact that popular sovereignty is still, as much as in the days of Napoleon I, the primary characteristic of the nation. The principles of liberalism, with astonishing adaptability, continue to reign as supreme as in 1810 when Napoleon made plans for his chilling decree for the suspension of personal freedom with the reservation, "There ought to be a couple of pages of guarded reasoning, well seasoned with liberal ideas [in order to make it palatable]."[84]

Already, under the First Empire, France had experienced "a government that was more powerful and much more absolutist than the one the Revolution toppled, a government that grasped all power and concentrated it in itself, eliminating every dearly-bought freedom and replacing them with sham copies. By popular sovereignty it meant no more than the votes of those who had no way of informing themselves, who were denied means of concerted action, and who ultimately had

---

[84] Baron Pelet de la Lozère, *Napoleon in Council*, trans. Basil Hall (Edinburgh, Robert Cadell, 1837), p. 218.

no power of choice. And, while robbing the nation of its ability to govern itself, and of the basic securities of law, and of the freedom to think, write and speak—that is, of the most precious and worthy victories of 1789—it still dared to assume that great name."[85]

The intensity of this absolutism corresponded to the degree of opposition it encountered. Long ago Chateaubriand[86] wrote: "One detects a kind of lethargy among men in our country that seduces them into apathy." When we are reduced to helplessness, when we cave in and resign ourselves, "we withdraw into a narrow individualism where all public virtue is stifled," and the heaviest yoke appears mild. But if we want to revel in it, we have to forget that—even as we bask in its seeming mildness—its power is unlimited, its energies adapted to the requirements of the moment, and its motto of "The Public Weal" authorises and justifies everything that serves to crush its opponents.

The base nature of this obedience testifies to the despondency of our time. The agitations of liberalism, at least, attest "the impossibility of a Christian nation ever endorsing a merely human power that consults only its own interest and rules only for its own ends."[87] But such noble repugnance has now disappeared. We submit, we cower; but we cannot forget that such obedience is quite different from that of our forebears. What matters is not so much the extent, as the character of

---

[85]Tocqueville, *The State of Society in France before the Revolution of 1789*, 3rd ed., (London: John Murray, 1888), p. 12.

[86]Chateaubriand, François René de, "De la restauration et de la monarchie élective" [Of the Restoration and Elective Monarchy], in *Œuvres complètes* [Complete Works], vol. XXV (Paris: Pourrat Frères, 1836), p. 341. Chateaubriand (1768–1848) was a French Catholic politician, diplomat, writer and historian.

[87]F. R. de Lamennais, "Des Prògres de la Révolution et de la guerre contre l'Église" [Of the Progress of the Revolution and the War against the Church], in *Œuvres complètes de F. de la Mennais, tome deuxième* [Complete Works of F. de Lamennais, vol. 2] (Brussels: Société Belge de Librairie, 1839), p. 247.

II. The Anti-Revolutionary Principle

our submission. "The baseness of mankind is, moreover, not to be estimated by the degree of their subserviency to a sovereign power; that standard would be an incorrect one. However submissive the French may have been before the Revolution to the will of the King, one sort of obedience was altogether unknown to them: they knew not what it was to bow before an illegitimate and contested power—a power but little honoured, frequently despised, but which is willingly endured because it may be serviceable or because it may hurt. To this degrading form of servitude they were ever strangers…. They loved [the King] with the affection due to a father; they revered him with the respect due to God. In submitting to the most arbitrary of his commands they yielded less to compulsion than to loyalty, and thus they frequently preserved great freedom of mind even in the most complete dependence. To them the greatest evil of obedience was compulsion; to us it is the least: the worst is in that servile sentiment which leads men to obey. We have no right to despise our forefathers. Would to God that we could recover, with their prejudices and their faults, something of their greatness!"[88]

As long as the Revolution exists, such absolutism and degrading servility is inescapable. Terrified of the complete breakdown of order, people will cheerfully embrace any power that can reassure them, even if it stifles liberty. Deliverance from that is worth any price. When the return of the Terror was imminent in 1799, what unexpected "deliverance" did people find in the 18th Brumaire! When the threat of communism surfaced in 1848, what a happy day was the 2nd of December! Hardly anyone asks how the victory was achieved or what it portends; all that matters is the sudden disappearance of danger. In a revolution, that's about the best we can hope for. But deliverance at such a cost will inevitably lead to fresh misfortunes: oppression at home, war abroad, tyranny and conquest lending each other support.

---

[88] Tocqueville, *State of Society*, pp. 219–220.

60   CHRISTIAN POLITICAL ACTION

So what should we do? What other possible solution is there to such an unbearable state of affairs? Once society has been levelled and popular sovereignty has gained sway, power—precisely because, by law, it is now simply executive power—must actually become despotic power; and it must make itself *irresistible* if it is not to be undermined. When Napoleon returned from the Russian campaign, he foresaw the resurgence of liberalism, and made a statement to the Council of State in words that assuredly lack neither truth nor profundity: "It is to *ideology*, to a dark metaphysics that has delved into the root causes of things and wants to erect the legislation of nations on its foundations, it is to ideology that we must attribute all the misfortunes of France. This it was that imposed on us the reign of bloody men; that proclaimed the principle of insurrection as a duty; that idolised the people by offering it a sovereignty it could not possibly exercise; that destroyed respect for, and the sanctity of, the laws by founding them on the mere will of an assembly of men ignorant of law civil, criminal, administrative, political and military, rather than on the sacred principles of justice. When called upon to regenerate a state, we must pursue principles diametrically opposed to theirs."[89] Thiers, however, was fully committed to his own view of things and laid the blame for France's misfortunes squarely on the shoulders of the conqueror's lawless ambition. And after reproducing the latter's philippic above, he added: "Such is the effect of one's faults, especially large ones! Apart from all the damage they do, they have the effect of driving to distraction those who commit them; and, amidst the mayhem they cause, genius itself seems no more than an angry child."[90]

---

[89] *Œuvres de Napoléon Bonaparte, Tome Sixième* [Works of Napoleon Bonaparte, Volume 6] (Paris: C.L.F. Panckoucke, 1821), p. 88, adapted.

[90] A. Theirs, *Histoire du Consulat et de l'Empire faisant suite à l'Histoire de la Révolution française* [History of the Consulate and the Empire following the history of the French Revolution] (Paris: Paulin, 1836), vol. 6, p. 775. Thiers (1797–1877) was a French republican historian and statesman.

II. The Anti-Revolutionary Principle 61

Unquestionably, Napoleon's statements are meaningless if they are aimed at philosophy and representative government. But if they were aimed at the Revolution with its sovereignty of reason and of the people, with its disdain for law and hence for traditional historic rights; or if they were aimed at liberalism; or if he was admitting that these unfortunate mistakes necessarily led to terrorism, propaganda, tyranny and conquest, then never did a flash of genius more brilliantly illuminate the history of the past. When liberal ideas dominate, Napoleonic ideas are not far behind; one abyss leads to another. Bonaparte's system is the immediate and legitimate heir of the Jacobin system.

Contemporary anti-revolutionary writers

Such political and social upheavals have produced significant and beneficial change in the world of ideas. This is not surprising. What had long been supposed beyond doubt, the extraordinary and salutary nature of the Revolution, has at least become problematic. When we are left with a choice between anarchy and tyranny, it is hard to be convinced that we are on the right path. "There are periods when, by the brilliance of events that interpret their times, God sheds such light on mankind as would enlighten and civilise every living soul, if our wanton carelessness and proud obstinacy did not obstruct it. We have lived, and still do live, in such an august time."[91]

Those distinguished historians who have encountered such upheavals and misfortunes as ours, in their immersion in the past, have not resisted the temptation of combatting—or rather have not failed in their duty to combat—the deadly spirit of revolution, through

---

[91] *Discours de M. Guizot: en réponse au discours prononcé par M. le Comte de Montalembert pour sa réception à l'Académie Française, le 5 février 1852* [Guizot's speech in response to the speech by Count de Montalembert upon his reception in the French Academy, 5 February 1852] (Paris: Didier, 1852).

striking and instructive parallels. For instance, we have Ranke[92] and his enlightening works. Then there is Macaulay,[93] with his *History of England*, that marvellous commentary on Burke's principles and the latter's defence of the "Old" Whigs who established the British Constitution against the "New" Whigs who advocated principles that undermined it; a striking contrast that Macaulay summed up in a single sentence: "It is because we had a preserving revolution in the seventeenth century that we have not had a destroying revolution in the nineteenth."[94]

Similarly, John Lothrop Motley, the writer who so admirably popularised, in America and Europe, the memory of those great events that, under the auspices of a hero and a martyr, brought about the Republic of the United Provinces, has highlighted the difference between revolutions in the ordinary sense and *The Revolution* in the unique sense, between *a realignment of powers* and *a subversion of principles*. He makes clear the consensus between William I, William III, and Washington, in their love of national historic freedoms. He draws a clear distinction between necessarily lawless revolution and the lawful and beneficial revolutions of the Low Countries, England and the United States of America.

The French Revolution, in all its various phases, but especially in its general ideas and universal trends, has now become the subject of serious and comprehensive study.

The events of 1848 have made the *Mémoires de Mallet du Pan* [Memoirs of Mallet du Pan]—collected and arranged with remarkable

---

[92]Leopold von Ranke (1795–1886), German historian, pioneer of the scientific method of historiography.

[93]Thomas Babington Macaulay (1800–1859), British historian and politician.

[94]Macaulay, *The History of England from the Accession of James the Second*, Vol. 2, ch. 5.

II. The Anti-Revolutionary Principle 63

talent by Sayous,[95] and published in 1851—of real significance for today, in addition to their intrinsic value. Every page of his correspondence reveals a deep thinker and a first-rate publicist who, already before he became acquainted with Burke's writings, had exposed and condemned the Revolution with the same wisdom and the same penetrating insight. I shall limit myself, albeit reluctantly, to a single passage, but one that bears the imprint of the accuracy and depth that Mallet du Pan applied to an investigation of the various phases and overall character of that fearful era. "The essential features of revolutionary doctrine never change. For each and every devotee of revolution this anti-social theory is a veritable religion. The revolutionary system can be applied to any nation; its philosophical principles are applicable to every situation and the foe of all government. Its authors respect England as little as they do an oriental despotism; they infect republics as easily as monarchies with their poison. Its fanaticism for irreligion, equality, and propagandism is pushed to the extreme; it is a thousand times more atrocious than religious fanaticism has ever been. And they all look to France as the home of their teaching and the heart of their union. It is a formidable sect that spreads and propagates itself like Islam: by armies and public opinion. In one hand it bears a sword; in the other, the Rights of Man."[96]

Mallet du Pan died in 1802. We turn now to works published, since 1848, by the instigators themselves. As an example we shall take Barante's *History of the National Convention*.[97] What do we read in the Preface? That which is so important to remember, and which we have

---

[95] André Sayous (1808–1870), Swiss professor of literature in the Academy of Geneva, entered the French government in 1848.

[96] Jacques Mallet du Pan, *Mémoires et correspondance de Mallet Du Pan: pour servir à l'histoire de la Révolution française* (Paris: Amyot, 1851), vol. 2, pp. 134–135. Mallet du Pan (1749–1800) was a French journalist and royalist agent.

[97] Amable Guillaume Prosper Brugière, baron de Barante (1782–1866). His *Histoire de la Convention Nationale* was published in six volumes (1851–3).

almost always forgotten: that the very success of the Revolution is what most condemns it; that outside the revolutionary coterie, no one opposed it; that such resistance as there was amounted to no more than a struggle of personal interests against sophisms; and that its antagonists emerged from the Revolution's own womb. "No opposition was mounted against the revolutionaries, at least outside their own circle. The experiment was pushed to the bitter end. The revolutionary notions had free course; nothing stood in their way or diverted them. If the enterprise failed, it must have been due to the fallacy of its principles and the perversity of its sentiments." Barante is in full accord here with what Haller wrote in 1816: "Every attempt to realise the philosophical system failed miserably. And it failed because it was *bound to fail*: because the system itself was false, impractical, and against all reason; and because the all-powerful force of nature opposed its implementation."[98]

Von Sybel's[99] *Geschichte der Revolutionszeit von 1789 bis 1795*[100] is one of those rare works in which the abundance of available material — which would overwhelm a common-or-garden-variety writer — has been a constant source of nourishment for an author of his perspicacity. I do not pretend that he recognised, in the Revolution, the natural and necessary result of irreligion, or "this overwhelming force that bends every obstacle…. [I]t has been correctly pointed out that the French Revolution leads men more than men lead it."[101] Even in 1789, he says, the Revolution was not inevitable. If the King had boldly

---

[98]*Restauration de la science politique*, translated by the author from the 2nd German edition (Lyon: Chez Rusand, 1824), vol. I, pp. 334–335 (ch. 11).

[99]Heinrich Karl Ludolf von Sybel (1817–1895), German historian.

[100]Multiple volumes and editions published starting in 1859. English translation of the first four volumes of the third edition: *History of the French Revolution*, trans. Walter Copland Perry (London: J. Murray, 1867–1869).

[101]Joseph de Maistre, *Considerations on France*, trans. Richard A. Lebrun (Montreal and London: McGill-Queen's University Press, 1974), p. 26.

II. The Anti-Revolutionary Principle

taken the initiative, if he had exercised his royal authority and decreed a doubling of the Third Estate[102] and the joint meeting of the three Estates in the National Assembly, as well as the complete abolition of the feudal system, many of the troubles would have been avoided. If, from the outset, Necker had acted with some dexterity, and those loyal to the Crown had seized control of the indecisive Assembly, the crisis might have been defused and the royal power strengthened, much as in the Danish revolution of 1660. Von Sybel forgets that by meddling in this way with centuries-old rights, they would have inaugurated the Revolution, not put a stop to it. He forgot that, when passions, coming to the aid of long-held principles, had reached the pinnacle of excitement, a popular movement was set in motion that nothing could resist. And he forgot that, by 1789, it had become impossible to arrest the implementation of a doctrine that had long held sway over public opinion, and that was regarded as a social Gospel.

Notwithstanding his error, von Sybel nicely demonstrates how the tide of human rights and popular sovereignty, through weariness of anarchy, finally took refuge in despotism and how, in its aspirations for a chimerical equality, inevitably ended in a social republic and the abolition of property. He points out the natural links between the parties that emerged from it, the ties that bound them together, the principle that gave them birth; a revolutionary tree spreading its branches. His honest and detailed account put paid to many a false assumption that had blamed the royalists and their allies for what are called the extravagances and excesses of the Revolution. He proves that the highly embellished and partial assertions made in this regard by

---

[102]French *tiers état*, Third Estate or commonality, excluding serfs. The other two estates were the clergy and the nobility. They convened and voted separately in the *Estates General*, so that the Third Estate was always outvoted 2 to 1. They called for a joint meeting and vote in a *National Assembly* in which they would form the majority.

Thiers, Mignet,[103] and their numerous disciples, are mere fables, grand myths of which the history of the Revolution is replete. He proves too, for example, that the aggressive coalition of Pillnitz was no more than a spectre, and that the war—which was the inevitable result of revolutionary propaganda—was a premeditated ploy of the Girondists to topple the throne. He demonstrates how diplomatic documents conclusively prove the testimony of the Foreign Minister, Delessart,[104] who was murdered [*couper la parole*] by the Septembrists: "My defence will surprise everyone, by showing what took place in foreign courts, by showing that one did not want war, and by proving that we ourselves provoked it and set the whole of Europe against us." Despite the forlorn hopes entertained by some of the émigrés and the indiscretions of the allies, neither the *ancien régime* nor foreign intervention were anything other than worthless scarecrows used by the Jacobins to justify their actions and continue on their course.

It will not do to try and pit Tocqueville[105] and his magnificent work—*L'Ancien Régime et la Révolution* [The Old Regime and the Revolution]—against me. He has shown how the Revolution, when its destructive work had been accomplished, returned in many respects to the path trodden for generations by the *ancien régime*. However, it was a reign of new principles that had arisen, despite the resemblance or identity of form. To give an example: "The first outbreak of the Revolution destroyed the centralised administration, that grand institution of the monarchy, but it was restored in 1800. And as has been said on many an occasion, it was not the principles of 1789 that triumphed, either then or now, in public administration, but rather

---

[103] François Auguste Marie Mignet (1796–1884), French historian of the French Revolution.

[104] Claude-Antoine Valdec Delessart (1742–1792), French officeholder under both Louis XVI and the revolutionary government.

[105] Alexis-Charles-Henri Clérel de Tocqueville (1805–1859), French political thinker and historian.

II. The Anti-Revolutionary Principle 67

those of the *ancien régime*, which once more took control of it and has retained that control ever since."[106] In the light of Tocqueville's profuse and enlightening exposés, there can no longer be any doubt about the resumption of the royal policy, or of its tireless efforts to strengthen central government by suppressing or neutralising local independent authorities by means of an administrative network. It is nonetheless true that the revolutionary logic, which had effectively destroyed every independent authority by merging them into a unified state, gave centralisation an intensity beyond anything it had previously known. It is true Tocqueville maintains that "The Revolution was not made, as some have supposed, in order to destroy the authority of religious belief. In spite of appearances, it was essentially a social and political Revolution."[107] Nevertheless, he attributes a large role to the influences which in our view awakened the Revolution. He points out that "in the eighteenth century unbelief was first and foremost confined to those who had the most pressing personal interests for keeping the State orderly and the populace obedient. Impiety was no more than a kind of pastime in their leisurely lives. The Church of France had become silent, those who preserved the old faith shrank from being thought the only ones still devoted to it and, recoiling more from isolation than error, attached themselves to the mob without embracing its thinking. The universal discredit that was attached to every form of religious belief at the end of last century exercised, without the slightest doubt, the greatest possible influence on the whole Revolution. It put its stamp on the Revolution's character; nothing contributed more to giving its appearance the fearful expression it displayed."[108] Add to this remarkable passage a sentiment Burke himself would not have been ashamed to own: "The Revolution became a kind of new religion; an imperfect religion, it is true, with no

---

[106] *The State of Society in France*, p. 110, paraphrased.

[107] *The State of Society in France*, p. 33.

[108] *The State of Society in France*, p. 283–285, abridged.

68 CHRISTIAN POLITICAL ACTION

God, no worship, and no after-life; nevertheless, like Islam, it filled the earth with its soldiers, apostles and martyrs."[109]

Although Tocqueville was a great admirer of 1789, he detected two distinct currents of thought in the philosophy of the eighteenth century: "In the one are found all the new or resurrected notions about the structure of society and the principles of civil and political law. They formed the substance, so to speak, of the Revolution. In the other, we have the purely fortuitous and irreligious current of thought that was spawned by conditions later destroyed by the Revolution. By its triumph this stream dug its own grave. From this perspective, the war on religion was therefore only a side-issue in the great Revolution, a fleeting if salient feature of its physiognomy, a mere by-product of the peculiar ideas, passions and conditions that preceded it and paved the way for it, but not an essential feature of it."[110] But he was assuming as incidental what in fact constituted *the nature and essence* of the Revolution. Tocqueville was never able to see what Burke had already seen back in 1793: "We cannot, if we would, delude ourselves about the true state of this dreadful contest. *It is a religious war*. It includes in its object undoubtedly every other interest of society as well as this; but this is the principal and leading feature."[111]

I do not want to pile up the quotations. I believe in the aristocracy of intellect, and intend to restrict myself to invoking the testimony of Montalembert,[112] Stahl, and Guizot.

Montalembert set little store by liberalism or its memorable calendar. Liberalism "wanted to date the world from 1789, and it muzzled the world precisely in the name of the ideas and principles of 1789.... The philosophers and liberals managed their affairs so adroitly that twice within fifty years their system culminated in the abdication and

---

[109] *The State of Society in France*, p. 22, paraphrased.

[110] *The State of Society in France*, pp. 10–11, paraphrased.

[111] *Three Memorials on French Affairs* (London: F. and C. Rivington), p. 172.

[112] Charles Forbes René de Montalembert (1810–1870), French writer and historian.

II. The Anti-Revolutionary Principle 69

the possible suppression of all law and liberty, and thereby to the applause of good people too frightened to take the lead! Yes, indeed; twice within fifty years the people, disillusioned for a while by the tide of evil and terrified by the outrages of the social machinery, laid their liberties in fetters at the feet of an absolute master. That, from the perspective of the present (1852), is what the triumphs of 1789 amount to."[113] And here's how he sees the Revolution's relevance for liberty: "I am not speaking of *revolution* as a *fact*, or as an *act*, or as a *passing storm*. I am speaking of *revolution* as a *principle*, as a *dogma*, as an *idol*. This revolution is not limited to a single country, or to a single time; it lays claim to every mind, and the right to take the place there of religion and society. It preaches the legitimacy of insurrection, always and everywhere, except against itself; disguised as democracy, it is merely a universal explosion of pride. And after it has obtained everything, it still demands more; insatiable as death, and just as implacable. I assert unequivocally that this *revolution* is not only not liberty, but its very antithesis. In victory and defeat, it destroys liberty; in the former, by suppressing it; in the latter, by instilling fear and hatred of it. It prepares the nations for tyranny, and fits them to deserve it; above all, it coerces them into resignation through terror."[114]

Stahl's works are so splendid and numerous that it would be embarrassing to have to make a selection. But if we wanted to fix on something characteristic of the man we would choose his speech: *Was ist die Revolution* [What is the Revolution]?[115] It provides a quick

---

[113] *Des intérêts catholiques au XIXe siècle* [Of the Catholic Interests in the 19th Century] (Brussels: Meline, Cans et Cie, 1852), pp. 50–51.

[114] Acceptance speech to the Académie Française, Feb. 5, 1852.

[115] Lecture given at a meeting of the Evangelical Association for Ecclesiastical Aims on March 8, 1852. The German original is included in Friedrich Julius Stahl, *Siebzehn parlamentarische Reden und drei Vorträge* [Seventeen Parliamentary Speeches and Three Lectures] (Berlin: Wilhelm Hertz, 1862), pp. 233–246. English and German ver-

overview of its origin, its nature, its course, and its results. The Revolution is a political doctrine that, since 1789, has penetrated the thinking of societies and their public institutions. It has subverted timeless legal relations. It has set up man himself as the creator and origin of the moral order. It has promoted popular sovereignty, unrestricted personal freedom, the levelling of society, and the rescinding of our traditional and historical laws. It wants to abolish all acquired rights in favour of public welfare. It condemns property as theft, all independent powers as tyranny; and the only government it recognises is one that, as servant and minister, is accountable to the sovereign people.

Illustrious leader of the doctrinaires, and until 1848 the liberal party's pride and joy, Guizot, "who has in our day so magnificently applied talent and science to the management of human affairs, is a statesman whose frame of mind and character have had the most decisive influence on his country."[116] The overthrow of the July Monarchy seems to have convinced him that the sovereignty of justice, reason and law must yield in practice to the sovereignty of the people. The ministers, who are the emissaries of this sovereign reason, are, as Berryer says, those whose authority is most contested, for they all see themselves as the mouthpiece of that reason, and so a huge bonfire of disputes is ignited by their conflicting personal opinions. It was experience—it seems—that taught him that authority must find its origin outside society, not in ancient and fallible theories but in submission of subject and sovereign alike to Him from whom all authority derives. Thiers parrots[117] "No liberty for the present, but it will come..."

---

sions are posted on the *German History in Documents and Images* website: http://germanhistorydocs.ghi-dc.org.

[116]Ernest Renan, review of Guizot, *Mémoires pour servir à l'histoire de mon temps* [Memoirs of the history of my time], in *Revues des Deux Mondes*, Year XXIX, Period 2, Tome XXII, July 1859, p. 179.

[117]A. Thiers, *Histoire de la Révolution française* (Brussels: Hauman & Co., 1840), vol.

II. The Anti-Revolutionary Principle

and Mignet looks for real political liberty as the belated fruit of the Revolution; Lamartine is for ever following his dreams for a way of justifying his faults and stifling his remorse; Cousin insists that the only foundations for lawful authority are the interests and consent of the people, that the tragic experiences of 1848 have not undermined his principles but rather confirmed him in them, and that, though plunged as we are in darkness, these principles are still a star to guide modern societies and bring order and good out of the most chaotic enterprises, dominating every form of government and determining what is best for France and Europe; [nevertheless,] Guizot was not afraid to admit—despite his attempts to show that France did not fail in 1830 or 1848, and that its misfortunes were caused by the thoughtless resistance of men rather than liberal ideas—that he had been wrong in many respects. And with courageous honesty he admitted that a long train of disappointments and setbacks were the "direct consequences" of the Revolution.

In his historical works, his memoirs, and his political pamphlets, we encounter decidedly anti-revolutionary maxims, interspersed with noble-minded confession. We shall examine just two booklets: *De la démocratie en France* [Regarding Democracy in France] (1849) and *Nos mécomptes et nos espérances* [Our hopes and disappointments] (1855). Order had barely been restored when Guizot—now retired to private life but still, because of his abilities, involvements and influence, very much a public figure—wrote: "France needs to regain its moral foundations and strength; it needs to regain its faith in and commitment to fixed and universally-acknowledged principles. But the revolutionary mentality can contribute nothing to this undertaking. Its performance in the past, the forces it unleashed, the goals it has set itself, the memories it awakens, the language it uses, would do more to stifle and delay than promote it." The evil that Guizot was speaking of at the time was none other than democratic idolatry; revolutionary

---

2, pp. 556.

liberty and equality were destroying every social relation. "Chaos is concealed nowadays under a single word: Democracy. It is this idea that has to be extirpated. Only then will social tranquillity be possible."[118] In 1855, he did not hesitate to scatter the people's fondest dreams: he showed how the generous disposition of mind was the fatal error that led to so many mistakes and so many disasters. "There was, in 1789, a universal confidence in man's natural goodness and in his wanting to be good. He would almost always have done what was good if, instead of being given the liberty to do so, he had not been perpetually irritated, misled, and corrupted by the vices of his social institutions and the abuse of power."[119] He finishes with a summary of the lessons to be drawn from contemporary experience: "We have supposed ourselves to be better than we are; we have miscalculated the evil inherent in our nature. We thought we were stronger than we really are; we have not simply miscalculated the limits of our strength, but the rights of that sovereign power that governs both us and our world. We have left out of our reckoning those eternal laws that God gave us, and have foolishly tried to replace them with laws of our own devising."[120] And he closes with the following very significant sentence: "Above all, let us lose no time in abandoning the paths the revolutionary mentality has put us on; they all lead to the same abyss."[121]

Guizot's authority, and that of those like him, ought to secure us against the never-ending criticism that we want a government made up of the errors of the Middle Ages, the despotism of Louis XIV, and the ultraorthodox opinions of the puritan sectaries.

---

[118] *De la démocratie en France* (Paris: Victor Masson, 1849), p. 138.

[119] *Nos mécomptes et nos espérances*, p. 3.

[120] *Ibid.*, p. 28.

[121] *Ibid.*, p. 29.

The anti-revolutionary principle is none other than the Christian principle

Was I wrong to claim that the anti-revolutionary principle is nothing other than the Christian principle?

It is regrettable that, even today, many Christians, disillusioned by the promises of liberalism, nevertheless believe that they can take on board its principles, in whole or in part, to serve the cause of religion and freedom. It is regrettable that they have not discovered, under the misleading veil of seeming moderation, the identity of principle with a radicalism that strikes at the very heart of religion and society, thus making them the blind instruments of "the hidden power that irresistibly draws the consequences from the principle, never suspecting that they are engaged in its fatal development."[122]

The Revolution, or modern philosophical theory, undermines every law of human existence, because it undermines Christianity. Herein lies the peculiar character of our time.

Indeed, what we are witnessing is one of the most terrible phases of that perpetual and mysterious war of which Scripture alone gives us the key. The Bible, which contains the history of the past and the future, recounts and reveals the complete destiny of humanity. The plan of a just and good God for restoring fallen man unfolds majestically down through the ages. Under His almighty hand events are shaped and moulded to a single end: the formation of an elect people, a spiritual nation, saved by the blood of the cross, and of a church militant here below and a church triumphant in heaven. The Revolution is simply the systematic undermining of the church of Jesus Christ; and a genuinely anti-revolutionary resistance to it is simply a

---

[122] Abbé F. R. de Lamennais, *Des progrès de la révolution et de la guerre contre l'église* [On the Progress of the Revolution and the War against the Church], 2nd ed. (Paris and Brussels: Belin-Mandar et Devaux, 1829), p. 142.

perpetual witness to the Faith, in a form dictated by our time. It is the Christian principle in its lawful, necessary and timely application.

The history of a revolution, the starting point of which is contempt for revealed religion, and the outcome of which is denial and doubt, would find a worthy motto in Pascal's lines: "All who seek God apart from Jesus Christ find no light that satisfies or is of any use. Either they do not come to a knowledge of God's existence, or, if they do, this knowledge is of no use to them. Because all they can do is establish, without a mediator, their own means of communication with this 'God' whom they know without a mediator. So they end up in atheism or deism, both of which are abhorrent to Christianity, and equally so. In Jesus Christ we find all our happiness, all our virtue, all our life, all our light, and all our hope. Apart from Him, there is nothing but vice, misery, darkness, and despair; and we can see nothing but darkness and confusion in the nature of God and in our own nature."[123] It is equally applicable to state and society. If we follow the way of unbelieving philosophy, we can expect to find nothing but destruction and chaos at the end of the road.

Back in 1831 I had already said: "Liberalism can be fought effectively only by Christianity." I was accused of reducing political matters to sermons and catechism lessons. I was not surprised by this at the time; but since so many terrifying upheavals have since sounded similar warnings by their thunderous repercussions,[124] I admit that the tenacity of these prejudices have since taken me aback.

Do you want the ideas of 1789? Very well; but you must bring them in connection with the Gospel principle.

---

[123]Loosely quoted from Pascal's *Pensées,* sections 543–549.

[124]Stahl, recalling in 1854 what he had written in 1829, adds: "Dieser Ruf meiner schwachen Stimme vor fünf und zwanzig Jahren ist seitdem durch die Donnerstimme der Weltereignisse wiederholt worden" [The call I made with my feeble voice for five and twenty years is now echoed in the thunderous roar of world events].

II. The Anti-Revolutionary Principle

Do you think democracy is irresistible and should be embraced not opposed? Very well; but if you have to embrace the current state of affairs, do not use it to legitimise a new order of things, or force us to bow the knee before the democratic idol. Christianity can work with democracy as with any other form of government. But if it is imposed as an absolute and necessary condition of the social order, hailed as a revolutionary dogma, and opposed to God's law—whose eternal authority must be respected by every sovereign power, be it popular or regal—the democracy of the social contract will always find itself opposed by the Christian faith. The reign of this democracy will always incur the consequences to society described in the chapter wherein de Tocqueville criticises democracy (devastatingly so, according to Vinet) for having sanitised despotism through the creation of the moral tyranny of the majority. "There will be no independence at all, either for the middle classes or for the nobility, for the poor or for the rich, but an equal tyranny over all."[125]

Serious-minded Catholics and evangelical Protestants have long and persistently proclaimed this irreconcilable conflict.

The Revolution began, said de Bonald, with the declaration of the rights of man; it can only be terminated by the declaration of the rights of God.

"Raise the sacred torch of truth above the ruins of Christian civilisation," said Lamennais, "let it shine before all men; let its beams penetrate the clouds of error and slowly illuminate those minds that have been led astray into false paths. Display before one and all the immutable principles of justice; elaborate the eternal laws, the unshakeable foundation of all power and liberty, until reason, despairing of its fruitless labours, finally understands that without Christianity there is

---

[125] *Democracy in America*, vol. 1, ch. XVII (in the Vintage Books edition translated by Phillips Bradley, p. 342).

not, and cannot be, anything but unrelieved error, chaos, calamity and bondage."[126]

The same idea was applied many years ago to the religious and political struggles of the time, as recorded in the *Journal hebdomadaire politique* [Political Weekly Journal] and the *Evangelische Kirchen-Zeitung* [Protestant Church Newspaper] of Berlin, as well as in the teachings and magnificent labours of Stahl, which are summed up in the following sentence that concluded a parliamentary speech in 1849: "the Revolution in Europe can only be brought to an end by Christianity, a Christian state, and a Christian school."

Down with the feigned Christianity of modern philosophy and theology! What we need is the positive Christianity of the last eighteen centuries, with all the well-known features of its history and teaching; we need the common faith of all the Christian churches. This is the faith Vinet called for in a few lines published in 1855, though written as early as 1832, prophetic lines so remarkably realised afterwards: "For a people without faith we can hold out no peace, no future but despotism.... Liberty without faith has brought down many a nation. If there are now free peoples who hold onto their liberty, who rejoice in it, who continually renew their energies with it, and who have nothing to fear, they are the peoples who believe.... There is no sure pledge of stability or liberty in a country where the masses side with the highest bidder or the most astute, be he anarchist or tyrant, and are prepared to bestow upon either (a tyranny by any other name) the fearful sovereignty of power."[127]

Returning to Guizot: No one has better highlighted the opposition and contrast between Christianity and Revolution: it is a matter of life

---

[126] Abbé F. R. de Lamennais, *Des progrès de la révolution et de la guerre contre l'église* [On the Progress of the Revolution and the War against the Church], 2nd ed. (Paris and Brussels: Belin-Mandar et Devaux, 1829), p. 94.

[127] *L'Éducation, la famille et la société* [Education, family and society] (Paris: Chez les Éditeurs [C. Meyrueis], 1855), pp. 79–80.

II. The Anti-Revolutionary Principle

and death. "If the Christian faith was more forceful, communism and socialism would soon be nothing more than obscure follies. If communism and socialism prevail, the Christian faith will perish."[128] De Maistre said that "original sin explains everything, and without it we can explain nothing."[129] Guizot does not waver in his insistence that the doctrine of the Fall implies the need for human laws and an authority capable of enforcing them. "The truth, as regards man's nature, is in the Christian faith; it is in man himself that evil resides; he is inclined to evil. I do not wish here to enter upon theology, but I use these terms without hesitation, as the most precise and clear; the dogma of original sin is the religious expression and application of a natural fact, the innate propensity of man to disobedience and license."[130] People are often shocked to hear the spirit of the Revolution described as anti-Christian. For them, the peak of exaggeration is reached in de Maistre's remark: "There is a satanic quality to the French Revolution that distinguishes it from everything we have ever seen or anything we are ever likely to see in the future."[131] Well, well! While doing full justice to the symptoms of greatness and the prospects of our age, Guizot wrote: "No one is more convinced than I am of the immense mistakes and fatal errors of our day. No one more fears and abhors the influence which the revolutionary spirit exercises among us, and the danger with which that threatens us; a human Satan, at once sceptical and fanatical, anarchical and tyrannical, eager to deny and to destroy, incapable alike of creating aught that can live or of allowing aught to be created and exist under its eye. I am one of those who think it absolutely necessary to overcome this fatal spirit, and to

---

[128] *De la démocratie en France*, p. 132.

[129] *Œuvres Complètes de J. de Maistre, Édition ne varietur*, 2ᵉ tirage (Lyon: Librairie Générale Catholique et Classique, 1891), vol. 4, p. 62.

[130] Guizot, *The Christian Church and Society in 1861* (London: Richard Bentley, 1861), p. 168.

[131] *Considerations on France*, p. 79 (ch. V).

replace in honor and power the spirit of order and faith, which is the spirit of life and safety."[132]

From the beginning of human history, the satanic spirit has told man: *eritis sicut Deus* [You shall be as God]. That is why, as Guizot said, our forebears in 1789 were condemned to abandon the vision of Paradise in favour of scenes from Hell.

The eighteenth century "was an age, not only of impassioned sympathy with, but of idolatrous adulation of human nature, and in this point especially it ceased to be Christian."[133] At every turn we are forced to recognise in the upheavals of our time the revolt of that human pride which deifies man and—boasting in its supposed independence—says of the living God, *We will not have this one to reign over us;* and of the God of revelation, history and nature: *I do not know you.* "What is after all, speaking religiously, the great question, the most important question which at present occupies the minds of men? It is the question in debate between those who acknowledge and those who deny a supernatural, certain, and sovereign order of things, although inscrutable to human reason. The question in dispute, to call things by their right names, between supernaturalism and naturalism. On the one side, unbelievers, pantheists, pure rationalists, and sceptics of all kinds. On the other, Christians. Amongst the first, the best still allow to the statue of the Deity, if I may make use of such an expression, a place in the world and in the human soul; but to the statue only,—an image, a marble. God himself is no longer there. Christians alone possess the living God."[134]

---

[132]Guizot, *Meditations and Moral Sketches,* trans. John, Marquis of Ormonde (Dublin: Hodges and Smith, 1855), pp. 15–16.

[133]Guizot, *The Christian Church and Society in 1861,* p. 172.

[134]Guizot, *Meditations and Moral Sketches,* pp. 5–6.

II. The Anti-Revolutionary Principle

Ultramontanism cannot successfully combat the Revolution

I am conscious of the fact that, in the struggle against the Revolution, Christianity has found eloquent defenders among the Catholics. Should we conclude that Rome is capable of effectively resisting the spirit of the age?

Certainly not. These apologists are only effective when, putting aside the distinctive features of their church, they appeal to the truly universal Christian church, in conformity with the old adage: *christianus mihi nomen, catholicus cognomen* [My name is Christian, my surname is Catholic].[135]

I am far from ignoring the invaluable services rendered by Christian Rome during the early part of the Middle Ages; whether to religion, by the spread of the Gospel, or to society, by raising a moral barrier against tyranny and by encouraging the birth and development of European freedoms. But a degenerate Rome; a Rome opposed to Gospel revival; a superstitious, unbelieving Rome; a Rome that claims for itself divine authority over the entire world and subordinates all temporal power to the will of a so-called Vicar of Christ; a Rome that at one time calls on people to revolt, at another makes common cause in its own interest with despots; a Rome that is the enemy of freedom, tolerance and knowledge; a Rome that is wholly incapable of either protecting or delivering Europe from the Revolution, and has twice already prepared the ground for it and opened the floodgates to it? Never! The fifteenth century was the prelude to a universal upheaval, when the Reformation stopped the revolutionary tendencies in their tracks. Three centuries later, when the complacency of the Protestant churches rendered them incapable of exercising their salutary influence a second time, it was Rome once more—the Rome that had dispersed or stifled the seeds of life and Gospel progress in France by the

---

[135] Attributed to Saint Pacian (310–391 AD), bishop of Barcelona.

violent exile and oppression of Reformers and Jansenists alike—that, through the scandal of its errors and vices, its intolerance and immorality, sowed the seeds that shortly sprouted into novel opinions and caused the eruption that was the Revolution of 1789.

Never forget that most of the abuses of the Roman Church are inextricably bound up with its doctrines, and that its so-called infallibility renders it incorrigible. Amendment would be tantamount to self-condemnation and abdication. Its innate character and bent drives it to give its errors unchangeable form and transform its false maxims into eternal principles. After an interregnum crowned with humiliation and misfortune, she was once more seen to be pursuing the course of her ambitious projects, boldly asserting her claims, and waiting for the opportunity and means for achieving them. Ever the same anti-Christian doctrines, the same contempt for free salvation, the same display of vain ceremony, the same Mariolatry, but with an added dose of idolatrous exaggeration. Ever, fundamentally, the same system of universal supremacy over nations and kings. Ever the same distortion of the precept, "Compel them to come in;" now interpreted as inquisition and torture, and culminating in a defence of the Saint Bartholomew's Day Massacre and the Revocation of the Edict of Nantes; ever harsh measures and religious *coups d'état*, setting a fine example to every succeeding generation. Ever the same resistance to civil and political liberty. Recall the Encyclical of 1832. It anathematised the "absurd and erroneous" maxim (or what the Pope called the *delirium*) that everyone should be assured of, and secured in, his freedom of conscience, and it went on to describe the freedom of the press as a fatal liberty for which it was impossible to express the full horror.

But, we are told, there are nevertheless Catholics who are both sincerely attached to their church and embrace liberal principles.

Liberal ideas they are, no doubt, but not principles of freedom. Note, too, that they do not use these to oppose the Revolution; they simply embrace its principles in order to further their ultramontane agenda.

II. The Anti-Revolutionary Principle 81

Still, we ought to be struck by this glaring inconsistency. How can we explain it?

To begin with, consider the Catholic who has sincerely and wholeheartedly embraced liberalism. If he gets carried away by the logic of his situation he may easily adopt the course taken by Lamennais: yielding to the current, abandoning church and faith, and summing up his apostasy in the antithetical proposition: "On the one side we have the Pontificate; on the other the human race. That just about says it all."[136]

Consider, next, those whose actions are calculated and geared to their personal interests. While many a Catholic was prepared to mount the scaffold for his faith during the Terror of 1793, we have recently witnessed clerics and laity in France following the herd and supporting the Revolution in all its various manifestations. This is not based on dubious evidence but on the unimpeachable testimony of Montalembert, who exposed the ridiculous and contemptible nature of the ardency with which any victorious party is always greeted. "After the February Revolution of 1848, a large body of Catholics, both clerical and lay, could be seen expressing their support for and delight in what they called a new era. In 1852, constitutions, debates, parliaments, and the control of legislatures and assemblies no longer provoked ridicule or contempt."[137] What did he think was the secret behind this astonishing turnaround? He certainly didn't think it took any special insight to root it out. "The high priests of violence and the worshippers of success think that, by going along with current events, they can mould both past and future to their fickle whims."[138]

---

[136] *Affaires de Rome* (Brussels: Société Belge de Librairie, 1837), p. 342.

[137] *Œuvres polémiques et diverses de M. le Comte de Montalembert* [Works polemical and otherwise of Count de Montalembert] (Paris, Jacques Lecoffre et Cie, 1860), vol. 2, p. 70.

[138] *Ibid.*, p. 71.

But we shall not dwell on these outbreaks of baseness, of which the Protestants were just as guilty. Rather we want to confront the main issue. Neither should we forget that, while the very nature of Catholic absolutism renders it incapable of successfully engaging the Revolution, an alliance of the latter with ultramontanism is no pipe-dream. History demonstrates that it is fully capable of allying itself with the Revolution and to some extent of merging with it, in the hope of eventually dominating it. At one time the Jesuits—preaching a radicalism for their own ends—had grafted the Pope's omnipotence onto the abiding and unchangeable sovereignty of the people as a universal principle applicable to all forms of society. Rousseau had already proposed such an idea, with the Pope as supreme president. The latter was to be servant of the servants of God, ruling over the kings of the earth through the sovereign people. In our own day, Lamennais has called for the absolute separation of church and state and put himself forward as defender of every form of liberty. He saw this as the only way of genuinely serving the cause of Rome, and of regaining the power it had lost on all sides. This could only be achieved by putting it in touch with the people directly, and by bringing about—through a lawless liberty—the triumph of the numerical majority; thus ensuring universal dominion by a clever detour.

Ultramontanism may, in desperation, temporarily resign itself to an abdication of its omnipotence and a share in its privileges. It may retreat within the boundaries of its spiritual authority, reinvigorate the system of the Middle Ages by adapting it to the exigencies of the time, and ally itself with the Revolution through its representatives and institutions. It wheedles its way into the Revolutionary governments, with whose support the people are thereby brought under the yoke of a twofold tyranny.

In different circumstances it may, in its own interests, hold its principles in abeyance. It kowtows to modern ideas, and looks on them as a necessary evil, but one from which it can draw temporary ad-

II. The Anti-Revolutionary Principle 83

vantages. Still, as the slave of false principles that are prone to undermine liberty, it is fundamentally opposed to anything that is consistent with the genuine and lofty nature or needs of the human spirit in the vagaries of current thought. It may conceal its antipathy, but it is not entitled to appropriate, nor can it, those verities that, interspersed with error, give the dazzling theories of liberalism the prestige that is so attractive and seductive.

I admire the spirit of freedom in the writings of Radowitz[139] and Montalembert, for example. They are, as Prévost-Paradol[140] says, "among those eminent and courageous spirits in the Roman Church who have preserved an understanding of and love for genuine liberty, though they have not been able to diffuse it there." He went on: "The Roman Church as a whole, and especially in the thinking of its leaders, seems animated by a contrary instinct. It dreads complete freedom for other churches and their complete independence from the state, equating these actions with persecution of themselves." And he gives a reason for it. "In its relations with the state, the ideal of the Roman Church is not independence, but domination; not freedom, but tyranny." Indeed, in keeping with its principles, if the Roman Church is not free to rule and persecute, it feels insulted and moans about being subjected to a Babylonian captivity. In his treatise *Des intérêts catholiques au 19ᵉ siècle* [Catholic Interests in the 19th Century],[141] published in 1852, Montalembert vigorously remonstrated with religious writers for betraying the cause of freedom in the name of their church; for putting themselves forward as advocates and eulogisers of absolute power; for rashly defending the Revocation of the Edict of Nantes against the Protestants; and for thus providing the latter with

---

[139] Joseph Maria von Radowitz (1797–1853), Prussian Catholic statesman and general, proponent of the unification of Germany on a conservative basis.

[140] Lucien-Anatole Prévost-Paradol (1829–1870), French journalist and essayist. The provenance of the quotation is unclear.

[141] Third edition (Paris: Jacques Lecoffre, 1852), pp. 123–124.

the perfect defence of their perennial claim that Catholic influence is incompatible with the preservation of free government. I do not believe Montalembert has any intention of concealing his principles to serve his interests; I believe he dreams of Rome truly embracing genuine liberty, but in this he simply is the victim of his own delusions. Nevertheless, convinced as I am that beneath this apparent union with liberalism there lie concealed designs perilous for us in the extreme, I would rather the enemy himself point out to me the connection between the consequences I fear and the premises I oppose. I would rather face the sincerity, the logic, the fury and recklessness of Veuillot[142] than the soothing words of Montalembert.

I know that some Protestant Christians—such as Guizot and Stahl, whose authority I generally respect—do not think that opposition to the ideas of freedom, tolerance, and progress are inherent in Catholicism.

In his summing up of the history of Europe of the last three centuries, Guizot issues some severe indictments of the ultramontane system. "Where Catholic absolutism has held sway, it has arrested and stunted social life; it has made nations unproductive; and it has stifled freedom. Any order it has managed to establish has lacked real durability and energy, and has been incapable of preventing times of great trial. When such times have come to pass, it has been found powerless against their excesses and almost as incapable of reforming as of maintaining itself."[143] However, when he addresses the very serious difficulties involved in any genuine control over the great intellectual powers, namely the nature of Catholicism and the conditions for its harmonious integration into modern society, Guizot thinks the Catholic

---

[142]Louis Veuillot (1813–1883), French journalist and author, popularizer of ultramontanism.

[143]Guizot's Introductory Essay to volume 1 of John Lothrop Motley, *Introduction à l'Histoire de la fondation de la République des Provinces Unies,* translation of *The Rise of the Dutch Republic: A History* (Paris, Michel Lévy Frères, 1859), p. lxxxvii.

II. The Anti-Revolutionary Principle 85

Church can genuinely and whole-heartedly accept, respect, and implement the principles of the separation of spiritual and temporal, and of religious and civil states. He thinks the obstacle is more historical than rational, and that it is the result of the past actions and former life of the two powers, rather than their basic principles or current relations. It should be possible, he said, for "a mild, intelligent Catholicism to flourish (as in France, Belgium, and parts of Germany, where it was not the instrument or controller of the civil authority) through moral activity, social influence and public prosperity."[144]

Where do we find this "mild, intelligent Catholicism"? Could it be consistent, logical Catholicism? When it is forced to compromise it comes up with any number of accommodations; but will the flexibility it exhibits under pressure still be evident when it regains its power and sees no need to bend anymore? Will the exceptional instance to which we willingly resign ourselves in the moment of peril become the rule? And should we look for Rome's principle in, for example, the conduct of the Belgian clergy in 1830 when they took advantage of Revolutionary freedoms and made common cause with it, or should we look for it in the Encyclical of 1831, which condemned them?

As for Stahl, he insists that neither the temporal supremacy of the Pope, nor the persecution of heretics by the civil power, is a dogma or article of faith for which Rome has claimed infallibility. These, he says, are secondary maxims that Rome could easily put aside. I appreciate the spirit of justice and fairness to the Roman Church, but I am wary of going down that path.

If Rome finally recognises, *in principle*, the independence and sanctity of temporal power; if it renounces the universal supremacy of the Pope; if it no longer claims the right to depose a heretical king, or to deny his right to the crown, or to absolve his subjects from their oath of loyalty; if the Bull of Boniface VIII, which declares that both the

---

[144] *Loc. cit.* Cf. Guizot's essay, "Catholicism, Protestantism and Philosophy," in *Meditations and Moral Sketches*.

spiritual and secular swords are subject to the Church, the former to be wielded by the Church and the latter for it, ceases to be the holy grail of omnipotence that Rome aspires to; if Rome conforms with the demands of modern international law and revokes its rulings that nullify everything in the Treaty of Westphalia relating to the tolerance of Protestants, a tolerance that its Congress of Vienna in 1815 deemed criminal and iniquitous; if the Catholic Church realises Guizot's hopes by restricting its infallibility to the religious sphere, that is to the relationship between believers and spiritual authority; if it disowns those who are regarded as its most zealous and sincere members continue to maintain—notwithstanding the course of events and ideas— that the rights of Christ's representative on earth are always the same, that subordination of all people at all times and in all places to the Pope remains the norm, that the independence of sovereigns is rebellion, and that religious freedom and equality are a reversal of the divine order; if Rome, in short, embraces everything it once anathematised, *then* we would certainly be willing to recognise this regenerated Catholicism, even going so far as to form an alliance with it in order to wage war, successfully and for the benefit of Christian civilisation, on the errors of the Revolution.

But so long as Rome refuses to pronounce its own condemnation, we should not entertain false hopes. When she needs our help, she will quickly enough stretch out her hands; but given half a chance, she will see it as her duty to eliminate us. And when the Revolution threatens and persecutes all existing beliefs with equal hatred, treating them all with the same contempt or even perhaps regarding them as the greatest obstacle to the development of humanity, clearly such peril puts an end to all Christian division. "Good sense tells Christians that they are all in front of the same enemy, much more dangerous to them than they can be to each other; for should he triumph, the blow will fall on each.... It will require all their strength, all their united efforts, to triumph finally in this warfare, and save at once Christianity and society."[145] The necessity for joint resistance, then, can result in a temporary union. But what Guizot does not seem to have grasped is that, by its very nature, Catholicism puts insurmountable obstacles in the way of a genuine and permanent alliance. Catholicism sees the Reformation as the seed from which the Revolution sprang. In its point of view it is right; and mark well, it is right not only in regard to pseudo-Protestantism, which is indeed simply the Revolution in bud, but also in regard to evangelical Protestantism. The Roman Church identifies its cause with divine truth and divine authority, arrogates to itself the role of official interpreter of God's Word, and recognises the working of the Holy Spirit only within its own circles. It confuses the sovereignty of the Scriptures (mediated through prayer by heavenly light) with the sovereignty of human reason, treats obedience to God as rebellion against its own so-called vicar, and maintains—on the assumption that atheism is consistent rationalism—that it is fair to say that Protestantism is no more than an inconsistent rationalism. For its part, the Reformation is ever mindful of what is false and lethal in genuine or ultramontane Catholicism and popery. Here, too, man replaces God. It is to *human sovereignty*—whether loudly proclaimed or artfully concealed—that Rome and Revolution, by their principles and along different paths, eventually lead. Against this two-pronged attack—against a system that is merely organised chaos in both church and state—the Reformation established once again the principles of genuine authority and genuine liberty, built the world of modern ideas on eternal foundations, and subdued the pride of man while satisfying his lawful desires. And this it did by proclaiming, as the basis of man's duty and the guarantee of his rights, the sovereignty of God and the law of God.

---

[145] Guizot, *Meditations and Moral Sketches*, pp. 22, 23.

The Reformation alone is capable of defeating the Revolution, provided it remains faithful to the Gospel and thereby confronts modern thought

Yes, for sure we can say: "For Christians of whatever church there is now a common cause. They have to maintain Christian faith and law against impiety and anarchy."[146] But if they are to be adequate for this task, nothing less than Christian truth is required, in its simplicity, purity and primitive force, that is, Biblical, evangelical, apostolic Christianity, the faith of the Church Fathers, the Reformers, and all who desire to know nothing but Christ and Him crucified, with free salvation through the blood of His cross. If we are to defeat the Revolution, we must have the Gospel stripped of all hindrances and set free from the superstitions in which Rome has sunk and distorted it. The Gospel is, and always will be, the ultimate anti-revolutionary principle. It is the Sun of Justice that, after every night of error, appears over the horizon and scatters the darkness. It destroys the Revolution in its root by cutting off the source of its deceptive reasoning. It thus removes those obstacles that liberalism by its very nature is unable to overcome. The rights of man (insofar as they are genuine and beneficial), the ameliorations, the advantages, which under the sway of the Revolution remain pipe-dreams, become realities with the elaboration of evangelical principles.

When wrested from a fatal amalgam, modern ideas are fully compatible with the Gospel. Rome opposes them, but in genuine biblical Christianity they have a place. If we want to possess the good things the Revolution offers us, one course of action alone must be followed: we must take up once more the work of the Reformation and continue in it. This is the one true way of destroying the Revolution's prestige and authority, of undermining its *raison d'être* and uprooting it from people's minds.

---

[146] Guizot, *Meditations and Moral Sketches*, p. 21.

II. The Anti-Revolutionary Principle

With this in mind, we need vigorously to repudiate the pseudo-Protestantism that is the Revolution's natural ally. We have to be clear about what the motives, nature, starting point, direction and consequences of the Reformation are. In 1841, I wrote: "It is imperative that we have a clear understanding of the grand and holy struggle that has dominated modern history for a hundred and fifty years. There is a twofold need for such awareness at this time, when both Roman Catholicism and a faithless bastard Protestantism persistently endeavour to distort the leading features of such a Christian regeneration and render them unrecognisable, and to turn the latter into a mere political or social movement. By nature, the Reformation has no affinity with the essential elements of revolution; rather, it repudiates them. We do not go far enough if all we do is point out that it outlaws violence under all circumstances and has never been capable from its own inner resources of exciting social unrest. It needs to be said, too, that when the Reformation put the Christian principle—obedience out of love for God and as the servant of God—into practice, and when in every sphere it placed human authority under God's authority, it validated power by putting it back on its true foundation. It counteracted and suppressed numerous outbreaks of rebellion that were incited, especially towards the end of the Middle Ages, by a false application of Roman law or by an imprudent enthusiasm for the republican remains of antiquity." Indeed, there have been many Protestants, some of whom are sincerely attached to the Gospel, who are unfamiliar with the true nature of liberalism and who, because all they can see in the revolutionary upheavals are the excesses inherent in such struggles, consider it a mark of esteem to be able to draw parallels between the Revolution and the Reformation. I myself have always stressed the contrast between them. "We often talk of links between the Revolution and the Reformation. We shall try to list them. The Revolution starts from the sovereignty of man; the Reformation starts from the sovereignty of God. The former judges revelation by reason; the latter subjects reason to revealed truth. The former breeds personal opinions; the latter brings about a unity of faith. The former loosens social ties and domestic relations; the latter reasserts and sanctifies them. The one triumphs through martyrdom; the other can only sustain itself by slaughter. The one comes up out of the abyss; the other comes down from Heaven."

I dared to hope that these preconceptions would vanish under the spotlight of a serious examination. I went on: "We do not lack the means to put such errors right nowadays. Merle d'Aubigné is publishing his *History of the Reformation*, which is more than sufficient to dispel the prejudices of an almost total ignorance by its plainness and historical detail. Ranke scatters profusely the treasures of his science in works that are replete with a thorough exposition of the facts. In Germany and elsewhere there is a renewed interest in times past. So let us have faith; critical examination and integrity are all we need."[147]

Our faith has not been disappointed. Historical studies have dramatically altered the judgments of serious minds. Time and again they now insist that it is wrong to view the Reformation merely in a negative light. Take Guizot, for example, who once said in his lectures on modern history: "The sixteenth century crisis was not just reformist, it was *essentially revolutionary*. We cannot ignore its true character, whether in its virtues or its vices."[148] But more recently he has stated: "It was not just the shaking off of a restraint, but the profession and practice of a faith, which brought about the sixteenth-century Reformation and enabled it to succeed; in principle it was an *essentially religious* movement."[149] Rémusat, a Roman Catholic writer, has likewise

---

[147]*Archives de la Maison d'Orange-Nassau* [Archives of the House of Orange-Nassau], Series 1, vol. 1 (2nd edition), Prolegomenon.

[148]Guizot, *Cours d'histoire moderne: histoire générale de la civilisation en Europe* [Course of modern history: general history of civilisation in Europe] (Paris: Pichon & Didier, 1828), p. 22 (First lesson, 18 April 1828).

[149]*Pourquoi la révolution d'Angleterre a-t-elle réussi?*, p. 2.

II. The Anti-Revolutionary Principle

stated: "The Reformation principle was not a matter of a particular theory of the church's constitution, or of this or that doctrine of the Eucharist and the other sacraments. Neither was it a matter of the hatred of the excesses of papal power, let alone of a general spirit of innovation and resistance to oppression. Even less, if it were possible, was it a matter of the contest between faith and reason or even between free enquiry and authority. The principle behind this religious revolution was religious not revolutionary. It was the principle of justification by faith, and by faith alone."[150]

In the religious sphere, the Reformation was a revival that created the evangelical churches, and even had a beneficial effect on the Catholic Church. In the political sphere, we must now examine how it laid the foundations for the dominion of ideas that have since been wrongly considered the discoveries and successes of the Revolution.

It is often maintained that Protestantism is the spirit of freedom while Catholicism is the spirit of authority. This is not true. It completely misunderstands the foundation, character, and work of the Reformation. It never opposed freedom to authority. It certainly overturned an unprincipled pseudo-authority, but it re-established the authority of the Word and of the Holy Spirit. For this very reason, and on this very basis, it could safely allow a principle of liberty that rests on, and is governed and limited by, obedience to God. And in this way it, to a great extent, bestowed on us the magnificent array of rights and freedoms that the Revolution merely puts on display.

It was the Reformation that, in opposition to the claims of Rome, laid the foundations of an independent civil power. And it laid them not on the whims of princes but on the order demanded by God's law; not with any intention of legitimising arbitrary power, but to remind whoever wields power of his subjection to the God who has entrusted

---

[150]Charles de Rémusat, *De la Réforme et du Protestantisme* [Regarding the Reformation and Protestantism]. Extract from *Revue des Deux Mondes* (Paris and Berne, 1854), p. 40. Rémusat (1797–1875) was a French politician and writer.

him with it and holds him responsible for it. The sovereign is thus no longer the Pope's subject but God's servant. Sovereignty bestowed by the grace of God, together with God's law, are opposed—under every form of government, be it monarchical or republican—to the pretensions of ecclesiastics or to the fickle whims of a numerical majority. It is the basis of every sovereign's responsibility to the King of kings, and the ground of every subject's submission to authority, for the love of Him from whom it emanates. Thus, the separation of the spiritual and the temporal, the distinction between church and state, was not intended to establish despotism as the new fundamental law. Nor, as has been claimed,[151] was it intended to deny the eternal charter of rights and duties, by which every lawless and unruly power is broken. Rather, it was intended to subject both church and state, by restricting each to its own sphere, to the immediate power of Him to whom has been given all power in heaven and on earth; to lay the foundations not of an atheistic state but of a secular state, to lay the foundations not of state absolutism but of a state submissive to God's will: a Christian state.

It was the Reformation that gave precedence to the rights of the individual, by the nature of its principles and the dedication of its martyrs. Once power had finally recovered its foundation, "the principle of individuality," says Vinet, "received from the hands of our Reformers not so much explicit authorisation as irrevocable warrant."[152] It is the Reformation that now safeguards what is most personal and sacred about liberty, whether against every form of socialism—catholic, ancient or modern—or against the revolutionary notion of the state as the organ of the General Will, whose omnipotence effaces every public and private right.

---

[151]Lamennais. The reference is unknown.

[152]Alexandre Vinet, *Essais de philosophie morale et de morale religieuse* [Essays on moral philosophy and religious morality] (Paris, Hachette, 1837), p. 36.

II. The Anti-Revolutionary Principle

It was the Reformation that, by preaching and practising absolute submission to God's will, obedience to men in obedience to God, and resistance to man's law insofar as it disagreed with God's law, and by insisting on personal responsibility and independence, prepared the way for freedom of conscience and the right of free enquiry.

All verities and all liberties are intertwined; they arise from the same principle, and are merely different outworkings of it. It would not be difficult to trace the ideas of equality before the law—the only genuine humanitarian system—brotherhood, and nationality, back to their common origin. On Reformation foundations we could even establish public law, which is just the conjoint and orderly evolution of order and liberty.

Indirectly and by natural affinity, the Reformation has exerted an incalculable influence on legislative and political development, on forms of government, and on the security of liberty. Guizot drew attention to this sympathetic link in a piece about the history of England, but it is equally applicable to Protestantism everywhere. "The power of conscience was responsible for the audacity involved in bringing to birth new ideas and new goals. Religious belief stood in need of political rights. Enquiry began to be made into why we no longer enjoyed them, who had usurped them and by what right, and what was to be done to recover them. The burgher, and even the peasant, began to think way above his station in life. He was a Christian; at home and with his friends, he boldly probed the mysteries of divine authority: what earthly power was so exalted that he had to abstain from such considerations! He read in the holy books about God's laws; to obey them he had no option but to resist the laws of others; he had to find out the limits of their authority over him. He who would understand the limits of his master's rights must thoroughly understand their origin." Awakened first in matters of religion, the spirit of free enquiry rapidly spread to every sphere of intellectual activity. The Reformation drew man's attention to the nobility of his origin and destiny, and made him feel intensely how contemptible was his unbearable yet ready resignation to an oppressive yoke. It made him appreciate the blessings of a people's free obedience, of its participation in the administration of public concerns. It prepared the way and determined the path by which the modern state has become, or is becoming, a personal government and a matter of public interest.

We Reformed Christians of Holland are doubly obliged to acknowledge these blessings. More than any other, the Reformed Church has established model governments, where liberty—far from undermining power—has settled it on firm foundations. While we could write a book on the faults and failings of an extreme and intense puritanism, it is nevertheless indisputable that the great social improvements, of which Protestantism was the source, owe their origin to the Reformation. Not a Reformation that was "vacillating, servile, more attached to temporal matters than faith, suspicious of the movement which had brought it into being and forced to borrow from Catholicism all it could hold onto while still separating from it; but a Reformation that was impulsive, energetic, contemptuous of worldly considerations, fully committed to the consequences of its principles, a moral revolution undertaken in the name of, and with a passion for, the faith."[153]

Look at England. Consider America. An unimpeachable judge—none other than Macaulay—insists: "England is indebted especially to the Reformation for its political and intellectual freedom and all the blessings they entail." Bancroft,[154] a writer whose words carry the same weight, but with respect to the United States of America, has borne witness to the same fact, and with sedulous care pointed out how it was a thoroughly biblical Protestantism—transported to another hemisphere—that achieved the same magnificent results already

---

[153]Guizot, *Histoire de la révolution d'Angleterre depuis l'avènement de Charles 1er jusqu'à sa mort* [History of the English revolution from the advent of Charles 1st until his death] (Brussels: N-J Gregoire & V. Wouters, 1841), volume 1, p. 26.

[154]George Bancroft (1800-1891), American historian and statesman.

II. The Anti-Revolutionary Principle 95

achieved in Europe: "The English peoples became Protestant through the Puritans."[155] The same is true in my own country. The more one studies the history of the United Provinces, the more one has to recognise that a complete and rigorous Reformation—bold before men but in humble and absolute submission to the Word of God—and the godly inflexibility of the evangelical Protestants, were the cause of our popular freedoms, our national independence, and our prosperity. Freedom flourishes in the shadow of faith. *Hac nitimur, hanc tuemur* [with this we strive, this we will defend]: we rest on our Bible in defence of our freedom; this has been the motto of our Republic and its story. "It was the good fortune of England in the seventeenth century," wrote Guizot, "that the spirit of religious faith and the spirit of political liberty arose together there. The religious innovators had an anchor that held them, and a compass they could trust; the Gospel was their Great Charter; they humbled themselves, despite their pride, before this law that was not of their making."[156] And turning to the American Revolution, he added: "The moral seriousness and practical good sense of the old Puritans persisted in most of the American admirers of the French philosophers; and the mass of the American population remained profoundly Christian, and as attached to its dogmas as to its freedoms."[157] The gospel abounds in happy outcomes, while Revolution always ends in disappointment. *Why was the English Revolution successful?* This is the title of a speech by Guizot; a title doubly significant because it contains and implies another: *Why did the French and European Revolution fail?* It is a problem of immense import for our future. The author addresses the problem thus: "The English Revolution succeeded twice. I would like to explain what causes have been responsible for giving a constitutional monarchy in England and a re-

---

[155] Source unknown.

[156] *Pourquoi la révolution d'Angleterre a-t-elle réussi?*, pp. 4, 6.

[157] *Ibid.*, pp. 176–177.

public in English America, the enduring success that France and Europe have so far vainly pursued through the bewildering trials of Revolutions that have, for good or ill, been raising up nations or leading them astray for centuries."[158] The contrast is bewildering only in appearance. The fleeting advances and endless setbacks of the spirit of Revolution are but the necessary result of the weakness and impotence of man who has cut himself off from his Maker: "Except the Lord build the house, they labour in vain that build it. The fear of the Lord is the beginning of wisdom. The rulers take counsel together, against the Lord, and against his anointed saying, let us break their bands asunder, and cast away their cords from us. He that sitteth in the heavens shall laugh; the Lord shall have them in derision."[159] If political liberty is to be achieved, then Revolution, which is constitutionally opposed to God's order of things, must make way for the Gospel. All that the Revolution can look forward to is the perpetual agony of a Tantalus or Sisyphus: longing for the fruit he can never reach, or watching the rock—so laboriously pushed up to the mountain peak— roll back down again.

Pseudo-conservatism

The anti-revolutionary principle is nothing other than the Christian principle, the Reformation principle; it is nothing less than faith in the living God.

The religious question is the supreme question; the fundamental question; the question that includes and determines the political question.

We have to go back to the eternal verities. Nothing more, nothing less, will do. In my view, the Anti-Revolutionary Party is *the party of*

---

[158] *Ibid.*, pp. 1–2.

[159] Psalm 127:1; Psalm 111:10; Psalm 2:2–4, Authorised Version.

II. The Anti-Revolutionary Principle

Christians: "It is a party quite different from all others, precisely because it is not as such a party. It is a party that will never kowtow to the Ministry, whatever it does, or to the Opposition, whatever it wants; it will side with the one as readily as the other *with justice* and, if necessary, abandon both."[160]

For man there is ever only one path that is safe and lawful: it is the path of faith and of obedience to God's authority and revelation. We must return to it if we have been unfortunate enough to stray from it. And such a desire to conserve the tutelary foundations of society is in itself the spirit of genuine progress. We want no other return, no other *conservatism*, no other *reaction*.

There are two kinds of conservatism that we equally disapprove of.

First of all, there is the kind that wants to recreate the past, unaware that "every attempt to do so very quickly becomes a grotesque caricature, or that former days cannot be conjured up at will, or that even when it does think it is managing to do so, it only adopts their outward forms."[161] It exhibits a ridiculous and fatal attachment to things that are worn out and obsolete. It has lost sight of the fact that all that can be conserved of the past is what evolves out of it, and that whatever is truly living changes; and that the living is only known by motion and progress. This kind is sometimes of a mind to restore what the Revolution wiped out as abuses. It tries to repulse the conquests of the modern spirit, and undo the improvements that, despite the revolutionary spirit, have been good and laudable outcomes of the social upheavals: religious freedom, abolition of the excessive privileges of the clergy and nobility, equality before the law, reform of the penal code, the unifying of the civil code, political centralisation, and the routine involvement of the nation in the government of their affairs.

---

[160] Alexandre Vinet, *Education, la famille et la société,* (Paris: Chez les Éditeurs [C. Meyrueis et Co.], 1855), p. 75.

[161] Fiévée, *Correspondance et relations de J. Fiévée avec Bonaparte,* Volume 1, pp. xliv, 19.

Then there is the revolutionary kind of conservatism. Alarmed by the unexpected consequences of the principles it has adopted, it fights against them, but refuses to change its erroneous principles. It hesitates, but not in order to change course; it simply doesn't want to go forward. But this is no more than a station or halt from whence the car, after a forced rest and with the barriers now removed, rushes on again at an even more frightful speed. Neither do the governmental forms and exceptional laws behind which it takes refuge offer anything but a fleeting security, one that vanishes at the first whiff of danger. At every turn, in everything it does, it only proves that physical force and violence have to give way to logic. We have nothing but contempt for such an unstable and dangerous form of "deliverance." However, we have no desire for a counter-revolution; we want the polar opposite of Revolution.

I have often been criticised for using the motto: "In isolation lies our strength." This was not something that I let slip out accidentally; I have only used it after giving it very careful consideration. What do I mean by it? Simply that we are not a shade of opinion that with other shades of opinion make up a single party; we are a separate party in our own right; we are bound together by fundamental yet neglected verities, and by a *principle* that is opposed to a whole array of *opinions* that—whatever differences they might have or appear to have—are united in a common contempt for what we regard as the indispensable condition for social order.

Separation in this regard is absolutely vital. At the least, in any alliance with other parties we have to be extremely careful to avoid being confused with them. We run the risk of being side-lined or wiped out, of being drawn into their schemes. Moreover, we must remain aloof from the revolutionary current; and the authority of God's law must ever be our unshakeable standard, if we are not to succumb to the popular current.

Conservation and progress

If we set out in this way to defend the anti-revolutionary principle, objective truth, and historical continuity in the church as well as state, does this mean that we are confounding politics and religion?

Certainly not. The principles, interests, and dangers are the same for both. "The cause of civil authority and of the Christian religion is clearly common. Divine order and human order, the State and the Church, have common dangers and common enemies."[162] In the higher realm of general principles, it would be absurd to divorce religious truth from political truth. At this level, the struggle of both is against the same doctrine, one that is equally destructive of church and state, that is, of morality and law. We need to be aware of this connection and not attempt to sunder what are indissoluble bonds. We do not thereby sacrifice religion to politics, or politics to religion. Neither do we paralyse the living regenerative forces of society, or erect a barrier against the spirit of improvement and progress. Quite the contrary. We thereby ensure religion its rightful influence. We bestow on an enlightened politics a renewed vision. We pave the way for genuine reforms, and remove whatever stands in the path of their realisation by banishing the pernicious and destructive principle of the Revolution.

I have often been accused of not wanting progress. If by this they mean I don't want to proceed along a path fraught with danger and deceit, I accept the charge gladly. Abjuration of error is the first and foremost sign of progress in the path of truth. Before everything else, we are bound to repudiate doctrines from which so many mistakes and misfortunes have arisen. Furthermore, we have to restore our traditional law to its rightful place, and in the form in which it has been—

---

[162] Guizot, *Meditations and Moral Sketches*, p. 15.

so to speak—*crystallised* by the free acts of man under the guidance of God's eternal laws.

In keeping with this maxim of intelligent debate, I have repeatedly declared myself to be opposed to the principle of lawlessness and the precepts in which it is incorporated and made manifest. "Opposed to the fundamental sin and appetite of revolution, the sinful appetite for destruction, and the haughty pleasure of creating it. Opposed to the sickness that drives man to suppose that everything in sight—people and things, rights and facts, past and present—are just so much inert mass which he can arrange as he chooses and which he can fashion and refashion at will. Opposed to the error that proclaims the sovereignty of the people and sees in them nothing but a great conglomeration of individuals, so many thousands, so many millions, by the acre, and all bound together and represented by a single cipher that goes by the name, now of King, now of Assembly."[163] Opposed, also, to the absolutism of the majority. Opposed to the deceptive tyrannical unity that, in the name of the sovereign people, reduces the nation to a servile obedience under the yoke of a centralised administration, even in the most restricted sphere of local interests. Opposed to the destruction of all social distinction and rank, leaving society no shelter but that of despotism.

But while I rejected every seed of disorder and dissolution, I was confident in the goodness of the principles I profess and had no hesitation in declaring myself to be—on the basis of those principles—a zealous advocate of all useful reform, all natural development, all genuine lawful progress; as well as what promoted the advance of Christian civilisation, irrespective of whether it was for or against the currents of the time. I applauded the steady transformation of personal power in public affairs, the acknowledgement of republican feeling by monarchy in general and ours in particular, as well as popular participation in the legislative assembly. I welcomed constitutional rule,

---

[163] Guizot (provenance unclear).

though not in the sense of modern reformers who have no foundations for their chimerical theories, but on the grounds of man's nature and the history and institutions of the country. I welcomed written charters too, but those whose laws brought together, related and improved national and customary law, not those that merely exist on paper.

No one has desired the establishment of representative government—the natural development of the glorious history of my country—more than I have. For me, the sovereignty of the House of Orange, the final culmination of a centuries-old struggle for independent statehood and the rights of the people, has always been indissolubly bound to the constitution, faithfully executed and inviolable, even in the most threatening crises. But while not underestimating the importance of the safeguards of constitutionality, I looked to find the government's strength in the nation's goodwill, in its historical memories, in the dynasty's popularity, and in the energy, morality and devotion that had heretofore established and consolidated the Republic's authority. No one has been more committed to the freedom and integrity of the press in general, and the newspaper in particular. No one has so strongly condemned a timid conservatism that, acting under the motivation of fear and calculation of interest, has at times remained passive and indifferent and, at others, indulged in bouts of violence generally stirred up by its own inordinate fears and menaces. No one has shown himself more the enemy of bureaucracy, autocracy, and arbitrariness, be it parliamentary or royal; but despite my sincere desire to cooperate in political improvement, I have always been profoundly convinced that governmental forms and constitutional laws have no efficacy unless they are rooted in historic and divine law.

As far back as the memorable years of 1829 and 1830, when the diplomatic "arrangements" of 1815 and the attempts to eliminate national differences with a *pseudo*-unity of amalgamated governments led to an inevitable rupture for the kingdom of the Netherlands, I bent my energies to demonstrating the benefits and shortcomings of constitutional government. There would indeed be benefits from such a constitution, provided it was valued and complied with, not as an embarrassment, but as the surest way to establish friendly relations and mutual support between government and nation. I drew attention to the dangers of the personal style of government in which the King had hitherto engaged, and to the necessity of replacing the ministers—then mere instruments of the royal will—with a genuine ministry, an intelligent body independent of the sovereign, responsible to both throne and nation. It seemed to me that it was possible, even then, by not yielding to current thinking and by not resorting to mere administrative or physical force, but by taking into account genuine needs, legitimate complaints, national feelings, religious beliefs, and acquired rights, to rally men of good will, disarm the agitators, and surmount the gravest perils.

And when the King, who took account of the most divergent views, also deigned to take note of mine at times, I made so bold—at every opportunity and with respectful frankness—as to inform him that, unless there was a change of principle, there was no possibility of succeeding. I kept telling him: "There is one absolute requirement, Sire. For nothing that ought to be done can be done; there is nothing that will suffice, nothing that will be of any use, if you do not give up liberalism. You are currently its idol, but you will as surely become its victim. You have to find a way to separate a genuine and national constitutional spirit from the revolutionary spirit and engage it against the forces that now threaten you. You have to thoroughly isolate the nation from a circle that has been led astray by false doctrines. You have to throw overboard those notions you thought you could make use of to merge populations of the most diverse character into a homogeneous whole. Unless you honestly and resolutely follow this course, constitutional government, far from serving your purposes, will become the means, under the control of a lawless circle, for bringing about the certain dissolution of the Kingdom."

Above all, I tried to impress upon him, firstly, that the Revolution cannot be defeated unless we destroy the irreligious principle of which

II. The Anti-Revolutionary Principle

the Revolution is merely the logical result, and secondly, that if the currents of unbelieving radicalism are to be combated, politics must find an ally in faith: and not such a fleeting faith as the pressures of a menacing crisis evoke, but one that arises from deep within man's soul; not one that serves our need, but one that dominates us.

When I retired voluntarily from public life in 1833, I believed that the time had come to engage the enemy on another field. For a long time liberalism had been the prevailing opinion; it was all-powerful in the upper classes of society, and counted virtually every political figure, every man of the cloth, and every learned man and scholar among its ranks. Nevertheless I did not want to completely withdraw from active involvement. In 1840 I was called upon to engage in the discussions of the States General on the revision of the constitution. I immediately insisted once again on the necessity of a change of principle rather than a mere change of forms. I did not see how a change of clothes could heal such rifts. And in the long years when, relieved of the labours and concerns inseparable from participation in public affairs, I was able to freely dispose of my time and energy, I was pleased to join with my friends in removing, as far as we could, the obstacles that a timid liberalism erected against the progress of evangelical renewal in both church and school. There, and there alone, in my view, could be found the securities of a better future. By drawing attention to the common faith of Christians in the face of a hostile and irreligious philosophy, I tried to put on display the advantages evangelical Protestantism offered for the establishment and reconciliation of authority and freedom. History, which provides ample evidence of this, has also provided a striking example of it in our own land. The course of her history is a practical illustration of the Saviour's promise: "Seek first the kingdom of God, and his righteousness; and all these things shall be added unto you" [Matthew 6:33]. How can we despair of the future, when we recall the past! In the midst of many painful disappointments, faith and life have returned to the Reformed Church and presage better times. This regenerated church, in my opinion, must not become the tool of a political party. It must become the leaven spoken of in the parable: the only genuine means of advancing the kingdom of God in every sphere of life.

☙☙☙

Despite having completed my argument for the anti-revolutionary principle and defended our cause, I do not feel that my task is yet complete. You made no attempt to address the criticisms your friends direct against you, someone says. For many of them, who have no objection to the principle itself, clearly do not approve the application you made of it when, as an ordinary member of the popular representative body, you were in a position to influence the course of public events. By your use of novel institutions to give a Christian party a privileged position, by your misguided imposition of Christian principles on parliamentary debates, by your treatment of every issue only from the standpoint of your ecclesiastical notions, you have helped to secularise the Gospel, and have provoked open animosity against religion, which has been compromised and discredited by your pernicious merging of things. You have almost driven the liberals to become, or at least to appear, the opponents of Christianity, and to regard you and your friends as enemies of the modern state. Your stubborn determination to drag religion into the political arena has merely led to endless misunderstandings, provoked pointless debate, and rendered all your labours vain.

Let us see if our parliamentary conduct warrants, in whole or in part, such a serious accusation.

III. OUR PARLIAMENTARY OPPOSITION

An opposition of principles

About fifteen years after I had retired from public life, the Revolution of 1848 tore me away from my quiet life. In 1849, I was dragged back into the parliamentary fray. Under the pressure of political upheaval, the constitution had undergone considerable change. The leading lights of liberalism were at the head of affairs. In the special session of the Lower House of the States General for the revision of the constitution, the anti-revolutionary principle was defended with integrity and ability by my friends; but they were not re-elected in the direct elections, and I found myself alone in the new assembly.

I reflected on the adage *Tu ne cede malis, sed contra audentior ito quam fortuna sinet.*[164] I saw myself as being especially called upon, on account of this solitary position, to make a determined stand that was fully consistent with our convictions, and to remind myself—with a lively sense of my weakness—that the truth is powerful and that even a single representative faithful to the principle forms the seed of a party.

As soon as I was presented with the opportunity, I had no hesitation in resolutely flying our flag. We are divided into three parties, the Minister of Justice said in the House: reactionary conservatives, moderate progressives, and extreme progressives. No, I answered, your calculations are wrong. These are just shades of opinion; the different but inevitable applications of the one anarchic principle; three opinions that revolutionary activity always brings to the surface: Movement, Resistance, and Via Media. None of you can reconcile order and

---

[164] "Do not yield to misfortunes, but, on the contrary, resist them with increasing firmness." Virgil, *Aeneid*, book VI.

freedom, and your disagreement is about the means for resolving the problem. It haunts you. But at bottom you are all of one mind in opposing the immutable laws of society, and on that account you are our common enemy. There are really only two parties: yours, which in one way or another serves the Revolution; and ours, which opposes it in all its manifestations.

My opposition, which I announced with this battle cry, was systematic. It was not an opposition that merely indulged in criticising; rather, while essaying at every opportunity to support and praise whatever was good in its opponents, it was an opposition unwavering and uncompromising on matters that were distinctive and fundamental.

It was a matter of principle, not of this or that ministry.

If I was to determine rightly the nature of my political actions and set their goal, I had to guard myself against some dangerous illusions, especially in such a neglected state of affairs. "To see things as they really are, is the first and foremost feature of the political mind. It implies a further feature, no less grand, that in learning to see things only as they really are, we learn also to aim only at the possible. An accurate assessment of the facts leads to moderation in setting goals and making claims."[165]

What did I want to do, and how did I go about it?

First and foremost, I intended to take full advantage of the platform and resources of the periodical press to make known the truth in all its bearings. I saw—and foresaw—after the events of 1848, further great disappointments; the expectations of liberty together with the promises made for it were bound to lead, in the ensuing chaos, to a strong reaction and to unprincipled proceedings ineffectually disguised. In the name of freedom we had introduced licence; to restore order, we were going to sacrifice freedom. I set myself to learn from these les-

---

[165] Guizot, *De la démocratie en France*, p. 142.

III. Our Parliamentary Opposition

sons from experience, and to report—in France, Europe, and especially my own country—the consequences of these insidious and disastrous developments, to trace them back to their true cause and deduce from them the great lesson of our time, which an anonymous pen summed up thus: "We have to find a better faith than what we find in the Revolution. Otherwise, for sure, we will eventually succumb to it. Over against the temporal, we have to boldly assert the eternal; over against revolution, those fundamental and eternal ideas that are an essential feature of man's nature and the world's structure."[166]

My aim was to attack the prevailing opinion by undermining its foundations. At the same time, and supported by my friends outside the walls of Parliament, I was not without hope of being able to exert a more direct influence on the important debates. But it would have been absurd at that time at least, to work towards undermining the ministry in an attempt to replace it. But, says Guizot, "It is a mistake to suppose that the struggle between ministry and opposition is a transient revolutionary affair, a momentary crisis the department must either overcome or sink under, and from which it must rapidly extricate itself by some means or other. Nothing could be further from the truth; catastrophic defeat is not the only possible outcome. The opposition does not simply exist to fight and hopefully topple an administration it regards as bad; its task is also to try, without undermining it, to force a change in its course, to make it exercise caution and come to a compromise, while leaving it in power. While the opposition does not hold the reins of power, it should not be completely devoid of it. It must always remain in close touch with the ministry, forever snapping at its heels and making it conscious of the need to not abuse its power. It must set itself to influence the ministry, despite its repulses and even its victories."[167]

---

[166] In *Revue des Deux Mondes*, 1849.

[167] *Des moyens de gouvernement et d'opposition dans l'état actuel de la France* [Means of government and opposition in the present state of France] (Paris: Ladvocat, 1821),

These were timely lessons for me. It seemed nigh on impossible to ever make liberalism restrain itself, let alone change course. The task was a noble one, the more so as I was going to be called upon to argue over organic laws. "Organic laws are so important," de Villèle[168] said in 1818, "that they must decide the future of the constitution. Done in a monarchical sense, they guide France and its constitution down a monarchical path; done in a democratic sense, such laws can smooth the transition from moderate monarchy to the most comprehensive democracy, from the genuine and common liberties of monarchy to the anarchic liberty of revolution, and from the rule of a King to the rule of a Chamber or Chambers."

I was not convinced that, in the political arena, liberalism would—in the first flushes of its renewed enthusiasm—give way at all. However, while I was afraid of raising my hopes and aims too high, I was nevertheless convinced that it was possible to arrest the progress of the evil, and that, most importantly, it was possible to relieve the Reformed Church of governmental control and to guard primary schools from the tide of religious apathy.

The constitution and its organic laws

When I swore allegiance to the constitution, some people were surprised, or pretended to be so. How could you of all people, the declared adversary of the Revolution, take an active part in public affairs in a regime that is the embodiment of its principles! My feelings in this regard at the time were identical with what I discovered later (in 1856) in an important chapter on the constitutional oath,[169] that Stahl added

---

pp. 304–305.

[168] Joseph de Villèle (1773–1854), French statesman and royalist. The source for this quotation is unknown.

[169] "The Oath to the Constitution and the Cure of Destructive Constitutions," ch. 6 of Stahl, *The Doctrine of State & the Principles of State Law,* trans. Ruben Alvarado

III. Our Parliamentary Opposition 109

to the third edition of his classic work on the *Philosophy of Law*. A frank and sincere adherence to the constitution, despite its regrettable shortcomings; but to the constitution, that is, to its requirements, and not to the aims and intentions that the various parties—rightly or wrongly—attributed to it. Adherence to the constitution, so as to scrupulously comply with it, so as to defend it against disastrous theories that would take possession of it, and so as to use the right of legal review, freely and as circumstance permitted or made desirable. Unswerving devotion to the constitution, sacred alike to King and people. *Coups d'état* have never seemed justifiable to me. The sovereign's obligations to the state's constitutional laws are absolute: he is bound to maintain them, even when he disagrees with them. To give the established order no other security than the King's personal judgement is to say that it rests entirely with him—with conscience as his only rule and guide—to determine whether there is a need to suspend, or even summarily repeal, on his own authority, in whole or in part, the constitutional provisions. In essence, it is to accept the constitution as his gift and to instate absolutism. As far back as 1829, when circumstances seemed to be forcing the King, in the face of a factious and violent opposition, to extraordinary measures, I repeatedly insisted, in private and in public, on the possibility of defending ourselves and of governing through the legal processes of a constitutional system. In 1856, one of the most distinguished members, of liberal views, Mr de Zuylen de Nyevelt,[170] bestowed on me a valuable—and, I believe, merited—encomium. Rumours and threats against the constitution had been spread abroad. I referred to such acts as culpable and dangerous. "I do not at all share the last speaker's principles," he said, "Nevertheless I acknowledge that, at this moment, they are our security against the dangers that threaten us; our security against a current of thought that

---

(Aalten: WordBridge, 2009), pp. 209ff.
[170] Probably Jacob Pieter Pompejus Baron van Zuylen van Nijevelt (1816–1890).

has been described as having little respect for our constitutional institutions; our security against a disease of epidemic proportions that has, for some years now, appeared to hold sway over Europe."

Organic laws of the utmost importance were put forward in the first three sessions of 1849, 1849–50 and 1850–51. They dealt with the right of association, ministerial responsibility, elections, and provincial and municipal laws. During these years the major issues relating to the sovereignty of the House of Orange, the nature and extent of royal power, general liberties and local rights, and the meaning and the scope of the constitution in its relations with historical law, were constantly on the agenda.

I was never seen to offer support to the friends of royal autocracy or personal government. On the contrary, I consistently argued that the King should rule and reign through a homogeneous and responsible ministry that would serve as an organ of effective action and, at the same time, act as a barrier against monarchical imprudence or impatience. However, I had no intention of taking part in reducing the throne to a mere focal point of the executive power, with the King as simply the secretary of a council of ministers driven by parliamentary pressures; or of subjecting royal authority, by means of a merely suspensive veto, to a majority of the electorate, to the legal establishment, or to the sovereign people. I wanted the royal authority to be wisely limited by a system of legislative power and by popular rights, but nevertheless sovereign in its own sphere. As such it would have that pre-eminence and legal precedence that—unless royalty is merely a form of democracy!—is the hallmark of a monarchical yet constitutional state. My loyalty and devotion qualified me to stand before a King who was listening to dangerous advice: "The constitution enshrines, *as a right*, the intervention of the country in the deliberation of public interests; this intervention has a positive effect because—ever bringing your government's public intentions and the people's wishes into harmony—it is the indispensable condition for the smooth running of public affairs." However, if I had adopted these words from

III. Our Parliamentary Opposition

the address presented to Charles X in March 1830, I would have needed to add to this otherwise unimpeachable declaration (if I wanted to avoid being unwittingly complicit in illegal schemes) a safeguard against its being given a liberal interpretation and motive, and against an intentional anachronism that confuses the medieval subsidy with a modern-day budget. Such an anachronism, applying—by a confusion of ideas, in its own interest—the adage *no redress of grievances, no grant of subsidies*, creates for itself a special law for finance by which it takes control of all power and turns a refusal to agree into a sword of Damocles that perpetually hangs over both throne and social order.

What's more, I have never desired to limit voting to the upper classes. On the contrary, although I might not have preferred a system of direct elections, I was of the opinion that an extension of the suffrage would help defeat oligarchic intrigues and hopefully create a genuine public spirit, as well as provide a broad base for constitutional government. But while I gladly ceded a significant involvement to democracy, I declared myself to be against an electoral system based on an abstract right of representation for all; this would be the first instalment of, the first step towards, universal suffrage.

Furthermore, I have never been a supporter of independent provinces. On the contrary: I had only to recall the deplorable dissensions that the want of a central, highly organised power gave birth to in my country, to understand that political centralisation is the essential guarantee of a state's unity and strength. Nevertheless, I am opposed to the despotism of a centralised administrative bureaucracy. I called for genuine provincial and municipal freedoms. I especially did not accept—under the guise of decentralisation—a greater concentration of power in the hands of the upper levels of the administration. Such power becomes increasingly intolerable, as Dupin[171] has observed: "If

---

[171] Apparently André Marie Jean Jacques Dupin (1783–1865), French lawyer and politician.

we do not contain liberty within reasonable limits, we will foster a tyranny that will even invade our homes and make us regret ever setting up a central power."[172]

Finally, I have never been indifferent to financial matters or political economy. Only, I said once and again, with the venerable and apostolic Chalmers (who has so energetically highlighted the connections between the Gospel and general prosperity in his writings and practical activity): "There is no well-being without morality, no stability without religion. Temporal blessings, the assured heritage of a virtuous and well educated people, exemplify the scriptural assertion that godliness has the promise of the present life and the life to come. It is wrong of the economists to so frequently dismiss the moral element, as being concerned with a higher level of existence. It is wrong of the majority of theologians to distance themselves from political economy, as if it was concerned with nothing more than crass materialism. Nothing less is required than their mutual support, to bring about a satisfactory solution to the great social issues."[173]

While I was happy to go along with liberalism in desiring a system of political guarantees and liberties, I rejected the principle on which it justified its maxims and actions. Thorbecke[174] who, by his superior abilities and forceful character, had become the acknowledged head of the ministry and leader of the liberal party, was decidedly opposed to all I held necessary and legitimate. What I opposed above all in his various bills was the democratic notion, the notion that, as Guizot said, we must eradicate at all costs. And this is precisely what Thorbecke would not, and could not, abide. He did not want to hear about the sovereignty of the dynasty; he wanted to subject the crown ultimately to a parliamentary or electoral majority; and he stifled all resistance and even traditional rights in favour of an omnipotent state.

---

[172]Source unknown.

[173]Source unknown.

[174]Johan Rudolph Thorbecke (1798–1872), Dutch politician.

III. Our Parliamentary Opposition

As far as he was concerned, centralised democracy was a *fait accompli* and binding. Nothing could be more natural than our mutual antagonism. For, if I stepped outside the circle of Popilius[175] he found it convenient to draw around me, I would, in his reckoning, be guilty of meaningless rambling; I was perpetually off at a tangent and, what's more, opposed to the spirit of our time and out of touch with modern reality. Accustomed as I was to such reproaches, I was hardly terrified, and refused to cower beneath his rod. I took the liberty of countering the spirit of the times with the spirit of the ages, and of reminding Thorbecke at times of the very remarkable and, from a revolutionary point of view, perfectly orthodox words he had written in 1831: "Wherever the spirit of revolution surfaces it tries to create something, and always with the same result. It claims to possess something it never had. It wants a present without a past; it wants a future but nips it in the bud. It used to fight against the establishment; now it fights against the outworkings of its own theories. But we have to carefully distinguish this spirit from the actual order of things that emerged during and after the Revolution. For the Revolution itself was played out within the historical course of events and was subject to its laws. In this sense, it has become a millstone round the neck of future generations, one they will try in vain to throw off. From the very ground ravaged by the Revolution, a new shoot is springing up, but on a quite different principle."

---

[175]This is a reference to the Seleucid emperor, Antiochus IV, who in 168 B.C. asked to withdraw to consider proposals presented to him by the Roman consul, Caius Popilius Laenas. Popilius casually drew a circle round him in the sand with his cane and "suggested" he might like to give his answer before stepping out of it. This is the original of the metaphor about *drawing a line in the sand*.

Many and varied opponents

From 1849 to 1851, and even more so in the years that followed, we encountered great difficulties and countless opponents.

The Catholics were against us, as were the political liberals and the Protestant liberals.

Catholics should have made common cause with us. "Whatever their disagreements, it is for all Christians of paramount importance and a compelling duty to accept and support each other as natural allies against this anti-Christian ungodliness."[176] I stressed this counsel of practical common sense. I warned Catholics, as I had likewise always warned Protestants, against getting entangled in the liberal way of doing things, either out of self-interest or from miscalculation. It was hopeless. There were times when we could have hoped that, having been made aware of the strength and vitality of our national Protestantism, they would not be indifferent to pacific considerations; but it turned out to be a false hope. Their distrust was too great, and their most influential party wildly flattered itself that it could find here a way of successfully applying principles it rejected elsewhere. It feared the dominance of a Protestantism that was taking on a new vigour in a sincere return to the beliefs of the Reformation. It thought it could crush it by means of a democratic system, and far from joining with the orthodox Reformed against the Revolution, it joined the party of the Revolution against the orthodox Reformed. "Transformed and softened by the influence of the national character, liberalism in the Netherlands is now quite a gentle thing," said one of its organs. Very gentle for sure, like in Belgium in 1829.[177]

---

[176]Guizot, *Meditations and Moral Sketches*, p. 23.

[177]A reference to the liberal Belgian opposition to William I, leading to the rebellion of 1830.

III. Our Parliamentary Opposition

From these so-called liberals—liberals as long as the supposed advantages of the theory overrides its bitter taste—we turn to the real thing. For liberalism in all its nuances was our natural enemy.

Political liberalism held sway for a long time in our country. It was the disciple of Montesquieu[178] and Rousseau, or, more often, of their disciples. A superficial knowledge of our history led to a confusion of our forefathers' spirit of freedom with the revolutionary spirit. French influence had moulded public opinion. At almost every turn we followed in France's footsteps, with a timid moderation, admiring the theories but hoping to avoid the excesses in practice. In principle, the ideas of 1789 were once more the catechism, almost without exception, of those who meddled in public affairs.

Among us, as elsewhere, there were liberals of various hues: there were progressives and conservatives; there were some who wanted to advance the Revolution and some who thought a measured reaction was called for.

The events of 1848 were to determine the success of ardent liberals; the extraordinary talents of Thorbecke were to give them, during his ministry and for some time after, a dominance more often than not unassailable.

Nevertheless the power of the conservative liberals was not to be underestimated. Their penchant for middle-of-the-road schemes, for half-measures, and for procrastination, was quite consistent with the national character. There were points on which we agreed. Generally also they wanted the sovereignty of the House of Orange and royal authority; a real monarchy, not a republic with a King. They were against the separation of religion and state; they wanted a secular state, not an atheistic one. They valued the historical element in the constitution and refused to break completely with the past. Because of this they could count on a lot of approval and support. Indeed, by their

---

[178] Charles-Louis de Secondat, Baron de La Brède et de Montesquieu (1689–1755), French political philosopher.

inertia, they often held the progressive party in check. They could have defeated it, if only there had been a way of getting along with us and working with us to achieve our common objectives. Unfortunately, the party was itself fundamentally liberal and strayed from the goals it had set itself. By its theories it uprooted the very thing it had set out to maintain, and succumbed to a principle that quite took all the edge off its fine sentiments. And, lacking any inner energy of its own, it offered us no more than a kind of bourgeois Toryism, whose interests—as it conceived them—always led it to take the side of whoever was in power. "Shortly after the revolutionary commotions, this conservative mentality somewhat became their accomplice; for, having been misled by false calculations and devoid of any honour, it found it more congenial to embrace them than fight them."[179] Indeed, it regarded the issue as merely one of how far to go in practice. But in theory it was revolutionary, and the party was carried away by the consequences it had hoped to avoid. The issue between it and the more advanced party was simply a family quarrel about changes of personnel and alliances to make or break a ministry. And at the end of the day it gained little from its victories. Thorbecke was opposed to it; challenging it and stripping away any power it had become his obsession, his constant preoccupation, the highest aim of his policy; and as head of the cabinet or leader of the opposition, this formidable opponent almost always had them under his thumb. It is easy to see why the conservatives, changing tack with circumstances, would adopt a highly volatile attitude towards us too. On rare occasions, when our support was seen as not without its benefits to them, they made sympathetic overtures: they liked the idea of working together where we had common ground on social issues and patriotic sympathies. But they were no less persistent in regarding us as taken up with superstitious error and outdated doctrines which, they said, would never be

---

[179]E. Renan (citation unknown).

III. Our Parliamentary Opposition

realised in practice, though our imprudent and untimely zeal for them would disturb public order and peace.

Several causes combined to make liberals of every hue persevere in their lamentable course. Elsewhere the spirit of Revolution encountered many and skilled opponents in the field of science. But here it was different. There was no serious engagement with political studies. Public education [l'enseignement official] was almost exclusively in the hands of the liberal party. Hardly anyone knew even the names of those works that, in Germany and elsewhere, had noticeably changed public opinion. Most were complacently stuck in the rut that a most benign and flexible liberalism had dug out. They looked askance at our ideas; they believed, or were led to believe, that we intended to intrude the distinctive teachings of a religious sect into politics, and that our ultimate goal was to make an extreme form of Calvinism and theocratic absolutism the leading articles of a revised constitution.

There were very few of us in the States General; from 1850 to 1853 we were only three. The anti-popery commotion of 1853 raised our numbers to an incredible seven. It shows that among the middle and upper classes at the time, our adherents were not numerous. Among the causes of this numerical weakness, we especially have to reckon Protestant liberalism. While unbelief was still not popular, some forms of it were widespread and, though they seemed innocuous, they were undermining the foundations of religion. They attributed to our forebears in their historic struggle for Gospel truth a concept of tolerance that was actually quite foreign to them, and they set out to imitate them by imposing on the Reformed Church an unqualified freedom of enquiry and a latitudinarianism that was wholly incompatible with affirmative beliefs. Our opposition to this subversion of our entire ecclesiastical system was attributed to pietism, mysticism, and I know not what insane zeal. For the most part, those Protestants who had any influence were anxious to protect both church and state against our dangerous devices, and by systematically shunning us made us feel the full effect of their intense disapproval. In particular, we were the target of the intense hostility of the greater part of the clergy. But we must be fair to that large body of pastors who, on various occasions, proved faithful to their duty and worthy of their calling. Generally speaking, however, the Réveil was essentially a lay phenomenon and the clergy its opponents. Many pastors were friends of the new "orthodoxy." Others, while not denying the faith of the Church, were happy in their carefree tranquillity and decidedly opposed to anything that might disturb it. They had no intention of being taken for intolerant reactionaries, or of being regarded as enemies of progress and enlightenment. They were all too easily offended by the frankness of the orthodox, viewing them with suspicion, aversion, contemptuous haughtiness, and not infrequently with incredible animosity. As for orthodox doctrines and practice, they were afraid of being tarred with the same brush. So they packed the consistories with liberals to keep the orthodox out. They gave a warm welcome to such colleagues as preached another Gospel but not to lay Christians who refused to engage in their deplorable religious indifference under the guise of Christian charity.

Chances of success

Even the certainty of not being able to succeed is no excuse for inaction and silence; for just when error and injustice seem irresistible, a stand against them is most timely. Nevertheless, despite so many difficulties, we had prospects of success for our very limited plans.

What was our aim?

In the state, we aspired to bring about the downfall of liberal principles by demonstrating that, despite a vain display of forms and guarantees, they could lead to nothing but perpetual oscillation between freedom without order and order without freedom. Our wish was to cooperate in the great and glorious task which I had summed up back in 1837 as follows: "May we yet see, not by sudden and violent transitions, but by the positive influence of a gospel spirit, the semi-revolutionary laws and institutions replaced by Christian principles!"

For this experimental demonstration everything was about to give us its support. The impotence of liberalism would be revealed by the comprehensive outworking of its rapid successes. Welcomed with universal acclaim, unopposed by the slightest resistance, and regarded by the greater part of Europe as a model, the Revolution of 1848, while not living up to its promises, had neither excuse nor hiding place; it was now more difficult than it had ever been to deceive the public into supposing that what happened could be put down to bad luck and not the natural and inevitable consequence of its ideas. Indeed, in this respect, the lessons of history exhibited uncommon clarity and force. The theory was rapidly worked out in the most absurd enormities: the destruction of the state, of property, and of the family, was required as the first step in building a better future; a system was promoted that sacrifices man's freedom and dignity to the quest for a supposed universal state of well-being. In France and elsewhere, anarchy and civil war, disruption and disaster, were the consequence. And before long the excesses culminated in an even worse disaster: the woeful remedy. We rushed to the opposite extreme; the popular tide flowed once more in its natural course towards absolute power; "and the devastating torrent was engulfed in the stagnant waters of despotism."[180] Thus were fulfilled, even more than in 1830, the prophetic words so well expressed by an anonymous writer in 1828: "While we maintain that the popular current and public opinion drive us towards republicanism, we are far from believing that an actual republic could be established in Europe on the ruins of our monarchies. But it is no less true that royalty could be overshadowed by them and the state thrown into confusion for a while, even going so far as to topple our lawful dynas-

---

[180] Montalembert, *Des intérêts catholiques ...*, Brussels, Mortier, 2nd ed., 1852, p.185.

ties; only for the force of the natural order of things to restore monarchy under new dynasties under the cloak of tyranny. Then the most cunning will rule, and we will be only too happy to obey.... Upheavals, civil and foreign wars, the loss of our good and brave dynasties, and ultimately a despotism of the sword, for which we will invoke heaven as a blessing, will be the consequence of these woeful errors."[181] Indeed, a grateful Europe admired the skill of the inheritor of Napoleon's power and ideas in taming the monster Anarchy, and prostrated itself before a power that could dispose at will all the prodigious resources of France. The Second Empire, despite its essentially peaceful programme and its supposedly disinterested policy, soon brought to mind, by its great military expeditions, Madame de Staël's remark: "Bonaparte needed war in order to establish and maintain his absolute power. He gave the French everything but liberty; but to provide them with those fatal compensations for it, he had to do nothing less than devour the whole of Europe."[182]

In our internal organisation, it was obvious that reaction would be the order of the day. Once they had seized the reins of power, our liberals cowed the royal authority with an exaggerated fear of popular commotion, overturned the social order to impose a chimerical liberty, and set about sacrificing real liberty to the demands and interests of their own system. Repression was to be the principal outlet for their energies. They would increasingly renege on their promises, and far from fulfilling the just desires of a nation where liberty had flourished under the protection of religion, they would be compelled to deny its

---

[181]*De nos Réformes des causes qui s'opposent à notre liberté politique, et des moyens qui nous restent pour acquérir une liberté raisonnables* [Regarding reforms of the things that oppose our political freedom, and the means that remain to acquire a reasonable freedom] (Leipzig: F. A. Brockhaus, 1829), pp. 266, 283.

[182]*Œuvres complètes de Mme la baronne de Staël-Holstein*, vol. 2 (Paris: Firmin Didot Frères et al., 1836), p. 447. Anne Louise Germaine de Staël-Holstein (1766–1817) was a celebrated opponent of both the French Revolution and Napoleon.

III. Our Parliamentary Opposition

historic traditions and ignore its most precious rights. The tabling of the first organic law—the right of association—would furnish proof of this. As the Committee's spokesman, I was able, with the consent of almost the entire House, to draw attention to a reactionary object in the proposal, namely, the intention of using this law to make it virtually impossible to exercise a freedom indelibly enshrined in the constitution, one of the most indispensable prerequisites of popular happiness and influence. I had declared beforehand that Thorbecke, who was now in the cabinet, could not, even with his ability and energy, prevent the tree from bearing its fruit, that is, the theory from producing its consequences. We would soon be convinced of it. Under his leadership, there was little freedom and a very strong government organisation. Everything had to give way to what was called the public interest. Centralisation became universal. The rights of corporations, the rights of churches, everything in fact, seemed, at least in principle, to have been brought under the government's heel. The more I admired the prudence and boldness, the shrewdness and consistency of this outstanding man, the more, year after year, the facts supported my thesis; even when liberalism has had men of great talents and great strength of character, even when it is not up against external obstacles, it always recoils from the inevitable downsides of its own theories; it takes refuge in the arbitrary; it has not the wherewithal to meet the real needs of society; it can hold the nation in thrall, but it can never take on the character of a *national* government.

Besides, the terrible events that a fresh revolution inflicted on France and Europe powerfully influenced historical and political research, and raised doubts about revolutionary infallibility. People began to see a connection between 1789 and 1793: the same tragedy or drama, but in different guises; the Girondins still being dominated by the Montagnards and overwhelmed by the Jacobinism to which they themselves had given birth; the sword always making its appearance to cut short the conflict of words and bring the disputants to their senses. What a great leap forward! Previously all contradiction had been virtually smothered under universal applause, but now it was possible for powerful voices to thunder forth, to speak with the backing of all Europe, to freely acknowledge past mistakes and admit the real cause of all our disappointments and setbacks.

As regards the state, we restrict our efforts—as well as our expectations—to preparing minds for a return to those eternal laws, which, when obeyed, elevate and strengthen, and, when disobeyed, disrupt and subvert. But as regards the church, we aspire to something much more concrete: we dare to commit ourselves, whether combatting caesaropapism or a faithless clericalism, to restoring her independence and liberty. In the religious sphere as in every other, the church had been subjugated by the state and handed over by the civil authorities to the intolerable domination of a party that, with the aid of a bogus regulatory body, could only destroy the unity of the faith. Theological education, primary schools, and the church itself, were at the mercy of both religious and political liberalism. It seemed desirable, and not at all fanciful, that we should attempt to remove this unlawful and preposterous yoke, though by lawful means, and restore to the Reformed people the Christian education and preaching to which, in terms of their church's liberties, they had a demonstrable right.

Once we had settled on this resolute line of conduct, we found ourselves with a potent force behind us: in the national consciousness; in the history of a people whose prosperity and greatness were so closely bound with its religious character; in the annals of a dynasty whose glorious destiny was so remarkably entwined with the defence of the faith; in the traditional attachment of a considerable part of the population to the faith of their forefathers; and in the doctrines of the Réveil, in which we cannot but recognise, across the centuries, an echo of our Reformation martyrs. So we were carried along by the sympathies of a considerable portion of our fellow believers, especially in the lower classes of society, where unbelief had hardly penetrated as yet, and where Gospel preaching was warmly welcomed. And while things were quite different among the middle classes, where even religious folk tended to keep their religion within the confines of the church and rarely gave any thought to even the most fundamental doctrinal differences, there were numerous exceptions to this dangerous propensity. In the upper ranks, we could rely on the approval and support of a large number of Christians who had embraced the Gospel either through the revival of the religious spirit in our homeland, or through contact with the Christian literature of France, Switzerland, England, and Germany. Some, too, came to the Gospel through science developed from a Christian perspective, others through the severe lessons of contemporary history, which demonstrated the futility of unbelieving philosophy and led to a renewed and zealous seeking of free salvation through the blood of Jesus Christ.

A religion can be national without being the state religion.[183] In numbers and influence, the Reformed Church was in a position to overcome every obstacle and repel every assault, if it was united and grounded in the faith. If we took our stand on its beliefs and traditions, we would be able to appeal to the vast majority of the nation. Our course of action, and our duty, was thus set out in front of us. If we made ourselves dependent on the party of conservative liberals and disavowed to some extent our special character, we could only expect to be broken and swept away with them at every turn. But if we remained true to our unique position, we could be the rallying point for the majority of the population, who were still hungry and thirsty for Gospel truth and who clamoured for their rights so that they could carry out their duties.

Moreover, we were more than happy to reach out to our antagonists in all that was good or true or lawful. In turn, even our most strenuous opponents were not indifferent to our alliance. They wanted to make use of it: the conservatives, to resist the radical wing's

---

[183] Alexandre Vinet, *An Essay on the Profession of Personal Religious Conviction and Upon the Separation of Church and State*, trans. Charles Theodore Jones (London: Jackson and Walford, 1843), p. 502.

recklessness; the liberals, to defeat the reactionary scheming of the conservatives; the rationalist Protestants, to combat the ultramontanists; and the ultramontanists, to protect themselves against a rabid antipopery. Our credit rose each time the Revolution, or the reaction to it, or unbelief or Romanism, caused them to appreciate, in their difficult moments, the nature and scope of our beliefs and backing.

Our party's influence increases

In the political and parliamentary sphere, we were opposed by an overwhelming majority. And so we fully expected our antagonists to enjoy taunting our weak and insignificant little party.

They were wrong though, and they didn't really believe it themselves. For they knew very well that we were actually much stronger than appearances suggested.

After one particular supercilious outburst in this vein in 1851, a member of the Lower House, who was not one of us but was well-regarded and later became Minister of Foreign Affairs,[184] said: "Why, then, if this party is as impotent as they say, is it subject to such violent attacks? Because it is actually not as feeble as they would like to believe. It is the defender of positive religious convictions that have permeated much of the country; in several other countries these convictions are predominant. Where such convictions exist and their defenders do not recoil before the great difficulties involved in sticking by them, a great force is at work. That force will continue to grow, and will become almost irresistible, if such a party has right on its side and is prepared to suffer oppression and injustice on their account."

The endeavours and reversals of the constitutional government, and the response of public opinion, more than once backed up this observation, especially during times of crisis.

---

[184]J.K. Baron van Goltstein (1794–1872), Dutch politician.

III. Our Parliamentary Opposition

In the elections between 1849 and 1853, our influence became more marked. Even though our numbers in the Lower House did not increase, the elections were making it clear that there was a considerable body of opinion in our favour. We were scattered across most of the provinces and had a majority in only a very small number of districts; our electors were unable to achieve success commensurate with their numerical strength. An anti-revolutionary candidate could remain excluded from national representation even if he gained more votes than the candidate who actually got elected. However, in many communities where one of us could not get elected, we were able to play a decisive role if the conservative and progressive forces were roughly equal. In 1852, when my own fiercely contested re-election was still uncertain, a Belgian newspaper[185] reported: "In any case, whether we succeed or not in booting him out of the House, it is now a settled fact that the number of pietists that make up the bulk of his partisans has increased in recent years in an alarming manner. It is now a party to be reckoned with."

The danger that existed of making our opinion the object of enmity or contempt was also evident in the instability of the ministry, despite every indication of impartiality and even goodwill on our part. In 1849, 1853, and again in 1856, we were accused, with some bitterness, of having contributed to the overthrow of the administration. If this accusation was premeditated, it was very harsh; for we were quite unconcerned about changes in personnel because fundamentally, despite their minor differences, the principles never changed. But if all they meant was that we persisted in a systematic opposition, we admit the charge. First of all, because the charge is actually a commendation: we were simply exercising our right and doing our duty. Secondly, because the intensity of the complaint implies a confession. You seem to believe that, if we had committed ourselves to a policy from which we had nothing to gain and everything to lose, you would have been able

---

[185] *L'Indépendance.*

to make headway against your opponents. It is therefore a fact on which we are both agreed. By their sudden and inevitable collapse, successive administrations have shown that, despite the undeniable power of liberalism, every ministry opposed to our principles and unwilling to entertain our wishes was short-lived.

Called upon to put the revised constitution into practice, the cabinet of 1849 crumbled after six months of embarrassment and failure. The speed of its decline was further evidence that, when the crisis of revolution remains unresolved in men's minds, all resistance to it is swept away by the agitation.

Let us look at the cabinet that succeeded it. It was, they said, going to usher in a new era of representative government in our country. Aided by circumstance, carried along by the tide of opinion toward the target of its efforts, guided by a statesman whose ability and character carried great weight in men's minds, the ministry of Thorbecke embarked on its experimental policy under the most favourable conditions and seemed, in fact, destined to achieve the archetypal and model constitutional state. Soon however, the damper had to be put on this magnificent prospect.

By 1852, people were shocked at having waited in vain for bills that the constitution required the national representatives to deal with in 1849 and 1850. In addition, the government suffered a severe check to its financial plans. But what particularly damaged the cabinet was the very legitimate fear that the modern principles of equality, of which Thorbecke is our most illustrious advocate, might simply usher in a new kind of absolutism, and perhaps even one of the most dangerous kind. People felt that the end result of introducing such principles would merely be to hand over the nation's most cherished interests to the caprices of whatever majority was in power. This omnipotent leviathan, which we know as the state, would devour and regiment every independent form of life. To abandon ourselves to these democratic ideas would be to set up a parliamentary dictatorship with no principle

III. Our Parliamentary Opposition

other than its own good pleasure, concealed under the slogans of public order and national security.

Even at that early stage we could see the need to get involved with the question of the church's rights. Legal charity and the secularisation of public education were the order of the day. Though the government changed the form of its law regarding primary education on an annual basis, its policy—mixed schools that take no account of religious differences—was hardly in doubt. In 1852, the bill to fund them offended the sensibilities of Christian charity by its directives and especially its motives, and was vigorously opposed. The ministry was visibly shaken. It was at precisely that point in time that the anti-Papist movement of 1853 sealed its fate. Some insolent expressions, issuing from the Vatican and highlighting the already well-known ultramontanist antipathy towards our glorious past, became the trigger, in its already sick condition, for its sudden demise. The situation was a godsend for the ministry. It could claim to be the victim of an honest application of the principle of freedom and equality of worship, and by overshadowing its crumbling condition this fortuitous incident made people almost forget the real cause of its parlous state, leaving it to sink gracefully.

And what ensued? Twice, in a moment of crisis, in 1853 and in 1856, opposition to the so-called Liberal-Catholic League swept us on the tide of public opinion to the forefront of the national Protestant movement. Twice the ministry, which these sudden commotions had given birth to, rushed to distance itself from us; twice it paid the penalty. The ministry of 1853 had announced that it was going to proceed in the opposite direction to the preceding administration. And once it felt secure, it rushed to distance itself from even the slightest hint of agreement with the Anti-Revolutionary Party, whose support—now no longer needed—it thought would compromise it. It was not long before it realised that this stratagem, which at first sight had appeared adroit and shrewd, had inflicted on it a fatal blow. It was defeated in the elections, and could only prolong its miserable existence by submitting, with astonishing alacrity, to the wishes of the majority in the Lower House and by a financial recklessness that put even the opposition's most daring plans in the shade. Among other things, it unexpectedly abolished the tax on the mills, incurring huge losses to the public purse. This provided some respite to an administration so obliging to its opponents, but it also inflicted serious financial embarrassment on both the state and the municipalities that it left behind. As for the ministry of 1856, on which rested responsibility for the law on primary education, it too turned against us; and its fate was no brighter and no happier than its predecessor's. It was meant to be the tool of those it ended up fighting against; it achieved the very thing its mission had been to prevent and, having no other reason to exist, promptly disappeared.

Now, did this influence of ours, which was considerable at times, have any legitimate basis? Were we right to make use of it and make our appeal to the nation? Apart from our partial and fleeting successes, was not such a claim, over against a fiercely hostile public opinion, simply evidence of our insolent and ridiculous arrogance?

There is a simple answer to these questions, which at first sight appear embarrassing. Public opinion is not the same thing as national sentiment. The one is transient, the other enduring. The one agitates the surface, the other penetrates to the core. In the kingdom of the Netherlands, the territory of the United Provinces (that cursed corner of the earth, as one Jesuit put it), Christianity and Protestantism have retained—in opposition to every change of government, every shift of policy, and every theory of unbelief and doubt—their deep roots. Precisely where the Protestant Christian interest was at stake, public agitation, fully aware of the real significance of our religious and political mission, provided irrefutable proof that we were the popular party, the real representatives of a historically-rooted nation that, in its distinctive features, the torrent of revolutions and systems was unable to extinguish. "In France," Prévost-Paradol wrote not long ago, "purely

III. Our Parliamentary Opposition

religious issues are unlikely to stir men's minds. It is especially in its relationship with politics that religion still exercises the prerogative of attracting public attention here, and we do not have to penetrate far into our religious quarrels to recognise that, when they do excite keen interest, it is because they are really party quarrels under a thin veil of doctrinal difference."[186] In Holland things are different.

Such indifference to religious matters is not general, by a long chalk. It is partly true of the upper classes, who are pretty much the same everywhere. It is also true of sections of the middle classes; but definitely not the lower orders. Constituting as they do the largest section of the nation, they have ever guarded themselves, unlike the higher orders, against any whiff of unbelief or rationalism. Among these folk things are quite the reverse. They have no interest in purely political debates; they don't understand them, and care even less. They have no interest in the affairs of government, and only take part in them when they involve religious issues. And then they take part with gusto; it becomes a matter of life-and-death; and they make it clear what they regard as their lawful rights. As soon as we grasp the essentially religious nature of the debate and recognise the true nature of the problem and the heady mix of obscurities in which those who fear the popular and national enthusiasm like to wrap it so they can ignore it, we become — or at least are on the way to becoming — master of the situation. If people are to truly understand what was rash and what was reasonable in our demands and in our expectations, they must always keep in mind the distinction between the people and the voters, and between the nation and those with the right to vote. Under any form of government we should keep the common good in mind and consider the interests, needs and rights of the people. Every form of absolutism should be excluded and, perhaps more than any other, par-

---

[186] Introduction to Samuel Vincent, *Du protestantisme en France, nouvelle édition* (Paris: Michel Lévy Frères, 1860), pp. xix-xx.

liamentary absolutism should fill us with dread. Even the constitutional and representative forms become the most detestable government, when by a legal fiction we identify the representative with the represented and absorb the individual wills into the legal majority; to do so is to put the most sacred rights at the mercy of the government's whims and encroachments. Far from blindly trusting to parliamentary opinion, let alone public opinion, there needs to be a constant concern for popular sentiment and instinct, especially in religious matters, those that affect the heart and conscience. In problems of this nature, social distinctions should have no consideration; wisdom, according to the apostolic witness, is given to the meek and lowly of heart. Here especially we have to take care not to violate the people's rights; they should not be provoked, by attacking what they hold most dear and most sacred, to desperate opposition and abandonment of their duty. Under the impress of these thoughts, I have never tired of repeating the warning that, here in Holland too, most politicians exhibit contempt in this regard, and that they do so at their peril. "Religious questions … secretly govern all the rest; their mysterious and profound effects baffle all calculation: by turns they fall short of, or exceed both hopes and fears; they put forth the most invisible and the most inevitable snare to worldly policy."[187]

The moderation of our demands and the justice of our complaints increased their force. You do not have the right, we said, to force the Reformed Church, by means of a state-created ecclesiastical body, into a religious syncretism that will ruin it. You do not have the right to restructure public education according to your own whims, or to banish religious education in schools and make them inadequate for the needs of a religious people. You do not have the right to use constitutional government to enslave a sizable portion of the nation and

---

[187]Vinet, *An Essay on the Profession of Personal Religious Conviction and Upon the Separation of Church and State*, p. 220.

sacrifice the lawful wishes of Protestants to liberal or ultramontane cravings.

By calling for the rights of all individuals and the historic rights of the Reformed Church, and that as inalienable, we became the mouthpiece of thousands of our citizens. This turned us into a strong, compact and determined minority, and we could congratulate ourselves on having imposed a measure of caution on the liberals and of rallying the conservatives ... and even the Catholics.

The conservative party looked like it might vigorously oppose us, but all too eagerly it distanced itself from the struggles and abandoned the field.

The weakness of the Protestants, their divisions, and their increasingly apparent dissolution, aroused and encouraged the Catholics to embrace liberalism as a means of achieving universal domination. But they take the opposite tack when you take away their hope by erecting insuperable barriers against their audacious plans. When they become sensible of the fact that Protestantism will not give in, and that, in fact, if it becomes exasperated by their vaunted boldness, it is likely to return upon them their just deserts, you will soon see the Catholics openly move closer to the orthodox Protestants in order to obtain, through their mediation and impartial justice, securities against the very principles of intolerance they themselves have practised so well elsewhere, but of which they have little inclination to be the victims. You will see not only sensible and intelligent Catholics but even the ultramontanists, beating a retreat from the onslaught of the Revolution by ranging themselves against liberalism and for the common faith.

How to explain the disappointing result of our action—and yet, no reason for despair

I cannot suppress a tinge of sadness, when I compare our opportunities and the means we had for succeeding in them with the actual outcome of all our efforts. I have to admit that it would be ungrateful of me, even humanly speaking, to say that we have laboured in vain. I am fully aware that an accurate assessment of the results is difficult; that in the realm of religion and morals we should recall the advice of a wise economist: reflect on what you see, but even more on what you do not see. I know too that when neglect of principles becomes a way of life, merely daring to advocate them is a great service and has untold effect; and if one cannot do a lot of good, one can at least prevent a lot of harm. And in many respects, but especially in our fight for freedom of worship and for the freedom of education, our contest was neither useless nor unappreciated.

However, even when these things have been taken into consideration, there is something surprising and enigmatic in the history of the orthodox Anti-Revolutionary Party, and in the way in which, for some time at least, it was incapacitated just when it seemed on the point of triumphing. In 1856 especially, there were strong grounds for hoping that, in the law on primary education, we would gain a victory of the utmost importance, that the separation of the schools would open a wide door to the evangelical influence on popular education, and that the House of Orange, remembering its history and providential mission, would fulfil the duty of constitutional monarchy to maintain the rights of religion and liberty.

Why was our hope disappointed? What brought about such a quick and decisive reversal? How did a setback turn into a sudden and general rout, in which the party appeared to vanish completely?

It is a difficult and sensitive issue, a serious question concerning my country's past as well as its future!

While not denying secondary issues, I have to admit that we caved in, not because of the strength of our opponents, but because of the disunity among Christians and the opposition of our friends.

It was above all errors regarding the nature of the church that led, in my opinion, to a disaster that will prove incalculable in its extent and duration; for they led to a misunderstanding of both the legitimacy and the timeliness of our efforts.

What was actually necessary for success? A coming together of Christians; a serious, conscious rapprochement among those who were deaf to the siren voices of modern theology, those who still clung to the authority of Holy Scripture and the fundamental verities of Christianity, the Reformation, and the evangelical Réveil. We needed to be patient with the disparate elements, not exacerbate them. Minds needed to be enlightened through discussion and debate, and hearts strengthened through struggle. Above all, if we were to achieve unity and agreement, we had to assert the exclusive nature of truth and its practical consequences; in the interests of freedom of conscience for all, we had to ensure that no one was allowed to disrupt the church by denying its beliefs; we had to remind everyone that, in a church that rests on a set of beliefs, we are called upon not to bicker over its doctrines but to be built up on their foundation, not to stage a clash of philosophical opinions, not to assemble a raft of mutually-contradictory opinions under the transparent veil of false forms, but sincerely to serve God in spirit and in truth, in the spiritual bond of a common worship.

It is just this very simple idea of the church that was being increasingly challenged and abandoned. The proposed axiom was a paradox, and the paradox became an absurdity. The church, it was claimed, is a common forum and meeting point for individual opinions, and the permanent residence of truth and error on an equal footing. In matters of faith, the church's rule is to have no rule. The only rule—either inside or outside the church—is freedom for all.

One can well understood how, under the dominion of such individualistic errors—"The Individualists' errors are a misbegotten product of Christian piety and the spirit of the age.... perhaps the most subtle of all those currently circulating among us"[188]—we were defeated on the two great issues of church and school.

It would not be without interest to unmask the process by which we gradually arrived at a church that had no confession and no doctrine, and where, we are told, it is perfectly acceptable to denigrate, betray, and even remove the Redeemer; and at a public school where Christianity is admitted only to the extent it upsets neither Jew nor Greek, and only in the apathetic state that is the last sad refuge of discouraged spirits after a long and useless struggle.

For the time being we have to confine ourselves to the task of not losing either confidence in our principles or our sense of duty. When we talk about our principles, they counter with freedom of conscience and the rights of the individual. And when we mention the future, they insist that our cause is lost for ever. Often, though, I am uplifted by the approval of a writer one might not suspect of having misunderstood the interests of Christianity and humanity, or of having entertained fanciful hopes. I am happy that I can quote him in closing.

Speaking of a church, much like the modern Dutch Reformed Church, whose unity consists in nothing more than the payment of its ministers' wages out of the same purse, Vinet adds: "Such, notoriously, is the thinking of certain energetic men of consequence. I blame them for only one thing: calling this anarchy an institution and this chaos a church."[189]

While noting the benefits of the development of individuality, he warns against merging "two sworn enemies into an imaginary brotherhood: *individualism* and *individuality*. To the latter, society owes all its substantiality, vitality and reality. The former is an obstacle to and a negation of all society."[190]

---

[188] Frédéric de Rougemont, *The Individualists in Church & State,* trans. Colin Wright (Aalten: WordBridge, 2015), pp. 13, 14.

[189] *Liberté religieuse et questions ecclésiastiques*, p. 224.

[190] *Études sur Blaise Pascal* [Studies concerning Blaise Pascal] (Paris: Chez les Éditeurs,

What's the point of trying to deny or play down our reverses! Sure, we suffered a defeat; the sudden defection of a group of friends made it inevitable. Nevertheless, in faithfulness to the Gospel, with feeble means, and despite what may have been faulty or blameworthy in our actions, we fought for a good cause; a cause of which, more than any other, we can assuredly say—*tandem bona causa triumphat* [ultimately, good will prevail]—that it gives us abundant consolation and holds out unshakeable hope. "We do not promise," Vinet goes on to say, "We do not promise [the public Christian] popularity, we do not guarantee him from all discomfiture; but he will call to mind that the germ of victory is concealed beneath every defeat sustained for the cause of God; he will remember also, that whatever may be the aversion of the wise of this world, to the counsels of Christianity, the world is so constituted, that the moment Christianity re-enters into the heart of its societies, its counsels will be followed, even without being accepted."[191]

Rue Rumford 8, 1848), p. 102.

[191] Vinet, *An Essay on the Profession of Personal Religious Conviction and Upon the Separation of Church and State*, p. 151.

INDEX

Ancillon, J.P.F., 53
Anti-Revolutionary Party, xv, xx, 35, 36, 39, 96
Arminianism, 22, 24
Bancroft, George, 94
Berryer, Pierre-Antoine, 27, 70
Bonald, Louis Gabriel Amboise de, 52, 75
Bonaparte, Napoleon, xi, 26, 44, 47, 51, 56, 57, 60, 61, 97, 120
Boniface VIII, 85
Bourbon government, 47
Burke, Edmund, 54, 55, 62, 63, 67, 68
caesaropapism, 9, 122
Calvin, John, xxi
Calvinism, Calvinist, 9, 12, 25, 28, 117
Chalmers, xviii, 2, 9, 112
Charles X of France, 111
Christian state, 10, 11, 34, 76, 92
Christianity, viii, xv, xviii–xxi, 1, 3, 4, 12, 16, 34, 54, 73–76, 79, 88, 104, 128, 133–135
church
    Anglican Church, 7
    disunity of, 133
    Dutch Reformed, i, xv, xvii, xx, 28, 134
    Free Church of Scotland, xviii, 9
    freedom of, xii, 32
    Reformed, xxi, 21, 22, 25, 28, 32, 35, 130, 131
    subjugation by the state, 122
Confession of the Free Church of the Canton of Vaud, 3
confessional party, xv, xvi, xix–xxi, 12, 14, 20, 32, 35

Congress of Vienna, 86
Costa, Isaac da, xviii, 13
Declaration of the Theological School of Geneva, 3
divine right, divine legitimacy, xi, 50, 51
Dordt, 12, 13, 22, 23, 24
    Canons of, 1, 14, 24, 26
    orthodoxy of, 2, 12, 20, 23
    Synod of, 2, 14, 23
Dupin, André Marie Jean Jacques, 111
Ethical school, 36
Fiévée, Joseph, 44, 97
freedom of the press, 80
French Revolution, vii
Gasparin, Agénor Étienne, 9, 18, 29, 50
Gaussen, François, 2, 30
Goltstein, J.K., 124
Groen van Prinsterer, Guillaume, i, xvii, 6, 40, 100
Groningen school, 12, 28
Guizot, François Pierre Guillaume, 9, 45, 61, 68, 70–72, 76–78, 84–88, 90, 93–95, 99, 100, 106, 107, 112, 114
Haller, Karl Ludwig von, 52, 53, 64
Hengstenberg, Ernst Wilhelm, 6, 10
Hobbes, Thomas, xi, 51
Hobbism, 43
Hoffmann, Ludwig Friedrich Wilhelm, 11
House of Orange, vii, xv, 90, 101, 110, 115, 132
individualism, xix, 14, 58, 133, 134

versus individuality, 134
Islam, 63, 68
Judaism, xviii
King Louis XIV of France, 53, 72
King Louis XVI of France, 64
King William I, vii, 41, 102, 114
King William II, 29
L'Indépendance, 125
La Revue Chrétien, xvii
Laboulaye, Édouard René de, xxii, xxiii
Lamennais, Hugues Felicité Robert de, 51, 52, 58, 73, 75, 76, 81, 82, 92
Larchevêque, P.-Tim., xxii
Liberal-Catholic League, 127
liberalism, ix, 41, 45, 47, 48, 53, 57, 58, 60, 61, 68, 73, 74, 81, 83, 88, 89, 102, 103, 105, 108, 112, 114, 115, 117, 119, 121, 122, 126, 131
Luther, Martin, xxi
Lutheranism, 10, 11, 12
Macaulay, Thomas Babington, 62, 94
Maistre, Joseph de, 52, 64, 77
Mallet du Pan, Jacques, 62, 63
Mariolatry, 80
Merle d'Aubigné, Jean Henri, vii, xxi, 2, 23, 90
Monod, Adolphe, xxi, 2, 15, 18
Monod, Frédéric, 5
Montalembert, Charles Forbes René de, 61, 68, 81, 83, 119
Montesquieu, Charles-Louis de Secondat, Baron de La Brède et de, 115
Niebuhr, Barthold Georg, 52
Nitzsch, Karl Immanuel, 11
Oldenbarnevelt, Johan van, 21
orthodox party, xv, xvii, xx, 6, 7, 32
Panchaud, Jean, 5, 6
Pelagianism, 23, 24, 30

Périer, Casimir, 48
Pitt, William, 53
Pope, papacy, 80, 82, 85, 92
Popilius Laenas, Caius, 113
Prévost-Paradol, Lucien-Anatole, 83, 128
Maurice, Prince of Orange, 21
Puseyism, xvii, 7, 8, 11
Radowitz, Joseph von, 83
Ranke, Leopold von, 62, 90
Reformation, x, xx, xxiii, 12, 16, 22, 30, 39, 52, 79, 87–94, 96, 114, 122, 133
Rémusat, 90, 91
Renan, 40, 48, 70, 116
Reveil, vii, 2, 12, 118, 122, 133
Revocation of the Edict of Nantes, 8, 80, 83
Rome, Church of, 33, 79–88, 91
 inadequacy of, to counter the Revolution, 79
 opposition to anti-revolutionary political agenda, 114
Rougemont, Frédéric de, i, xviii, 134
Rousseau, Jean-Jacques, 42, 43, 50, 82, 115
Saint Bartholomew's Day Massacre, 8, 80
Savigny, Friedrich Karl von, 52
Sayous, André, 63
Separation of 1834, 25–27
Socinianism, 24, 30
St Bartholomew, 8
Stahl, Friedrich Julius, 6, 10, 68, 69, 74, 76, 84, 85, 108
Stuart, House of, 9
subjectivism, xxiv, 16, 28, 45, 52
Sybel, Heinrich Karl Ludolf von, 64
Revolution, the, *passim*
Theological School of Geneva, 3

Thorbecke, Johan Rudolph, 112, 115, 116, 121, 126
Tocqueville, Alexis de, 58, 59, 66, 68, 75
Treaty of Westphalia, 86
Trottet, Jean-Pierre, xvii, 1, 2, 3, 4, 5, 6, 7, 8, 10, 12, 14, 36
ultramontanism, 80, 82, 84, 87, 124, 131

Veuillot, Louis, 84
Vinet, Alexandre, xx, xxii, xxiii, 2, 8, 10, 11, 15, 16, 75, 76, 92, 97, 123, 130, 134, 135
William I, Prince of Orange, 62
William III, Prince of Orange, King of England, 8, 53, 62
Zuylen van Nyevelt, Jacob Pieter Pompejus Baron van, 109

Made in the USA
Columbia, SC
26 February 2021